It Draws Me

The Art of Contemplation

MARY M. MCDONALD, PHD

Liguori
LIGUORI, MISSOURI

Imprimi Potest:
Harry Grile, CSsR, Provincial
Denver Province, The Redemptorists

Published by Liguori Publications
Liguori, Missouri 63057

To order, call 800-325-9521, or visit liguori.org.

Library of Congress Cataloging-in-Publication Data

McDonald, Mary M., PhD.
  It draws me : the art of contemplation / Mary M. McDonald, PhD. —1st ed.
    p. cm.
  Includes bibliographical references.
  ISBN 978-0-7648-2179-0
  1. Contemplation. 2. Spiritual life—Catholic Church. I. Title.
  BV5091.C7M38 2012
  248.3'4—dc23
                              2012014897

Liguori Publications, a nonprofit corporation, is an apostolate of The Redemptorists. To learn more about The Redemptorists, visit Redemptorists.com.

Printed in the United States of America

16 15 14 13 12 / 5 4 3 2 1

First Edition

DEDICATION

To the contemplative artists in my own family:
my dear mother, Pauline Murray;
her sister, Diane Maloney;
my grandmother, Millie McGarry;
and George Adomitis, Millie's brother,
who taught her how to read and her colors
and to always enjoy yellow leaves against a gray sky

Contents

Preface   VII

Introduction   XI

    Exploring These Traditions   XIV

    The Heritage of Lectio Divina   XVI

    The Heritage of Icons   XVII

    The Heritage of Song Dynasty Landscape Paintings XVIII

    How to Use This Book   XIX

    Let's Practice   XX

Section I

The *Lectio*-Inspired Prose of Thomas Merton   1

    Ancient Monastic Reading   6

    Reading for Change and Insight   8

    Merton's Unpublished Lecture Notes on *Lectio Divina* 9

    The Loss of the Interactive Reading for Wisdom   13

Section II

Icons as Writing the Word   21

    The Doctrine of the Incarnation "implicit in every line" 25

    "Full of spirit and vitality and earnestness and power" 26

    "Its solemnity was made all the more astounding by its simplicity." 28

    "Christ Himself, present in those churches"   32

    "True knowledge of Him, in some sense truer than I knew and truer than I could admit." 33

The Silent Artist   34

"The obscurity of the place where it lay hid,
and its subservience to higher ends"   35

Section III

A World in a Drop of Ink   37

Landscape as Sacred   40

Academies as Nurturing the Contemplative Life   42

Brushwork as Revealing the Essence of Things   46

The Artist as a Contemplative   49

Section IV

What Monastic Contemplative Artists Want to Give Us   51

Conclusion   61

Further Reading on Contemplative Spirituality   65

Bibliography   67

Endnotes   71

Sources and Acknowledgments   76

Representative artwork   A1 – A32

Preface

This book began with an idea from two authors that kept nagging at me: Theologian Bernard Lonergan, in his book *Insight,* and art critic Margaret Miles, in her book *Image as Insight,* both believed that if people had insight into some important aspect of their lives, they were most able to live out that new knowledge if they had a model or an image to bolster it. Miles suggested tearing out images from magazines that embodied it. I had just completed a book on insight in writing, and their idea was compelling. How much more powerful would an insight be if an image could help someone live that knowledge? Miles' book taught me that contemplative images or contemplative writings can actually shape us or draw us in ways that lead to understandings we might never have had on our own. They can literally shape us or sketch us because they speak to areas in our lives we need to address or develop.

This ability of language and art to help us learn is something I remain fascinated by, and as I turned from language toward images, I kept referring to the contemplative art that I had been most in contact with, having gone to the Abbey of the Genesee in upstate New York beginning in 1988. A student at Hobart and William Smith Colleges, where I was teaching, had asked me to direct an honors project on Thomas Merton. This project prompted me to attend an early meeting of the Merton Society held in Rochester in 1989. I was so impressed with the values of the group that I began wanting to write for them. I'd seen Sister Mary Luke Tobin speak there and could not forget her words about Thomas Merton—that he wanted all people to stand on their own two feet. Through my visits to the abbey with Brother Augustine Jackson, I learned much of the Cistercian life and eventually joined a lay contemplative group. His guidance, support, and—most of all—friendship are the basis for much of this book.

My degrees are in the teaching of writing where we want to understand the effect that writing has on learning, and so turning to the effect art has on learning was natural for me, even though I am not an art critic. Through this experience of monastic spirituality and my readings in art and religious heritages, I began to see that the training and values of the artists came through in a variety of contemplative cultures and that what was most interesting to me was that few people knew how rich these heritages were.

I moved to Ithaca, New York, to use the Cornell University libraries because they have such an excellent Asian collection, especially of art books. I was able to study icons there, too. I am very grateful to the librarians of that university for such fine collections and to their volunteer translators. Also, once I began writing for the Merton Society members, I was encouraged by a variety of people there, including Bob Daggy, Donna Kristoff, Pat O'Connell, Ross Labrie, and Claire Badaracco. Paul Pearson and Marke Meade of the Thomas Merton Center and Anne McCormick of the Merton Legacy Trust were very helpful. I am so grateful to Christy Hicks of Liguori Publications for her interest in this manuscript and her enthusiastic, prompt, and kind guidance throughout this publication process.

Several monks at the Abbey of the Genesee were particularly helpful for their knowledge about the monastic world that Merton knew at Gethsemani: Father John Eudes Bamberger, Father Francis Steger, Father Marcellus Earl, and Father Justin Sheehan. Professor Lee Makela of Cleveland State University provided much help with research into Chinese art. Professor Jennifer Visocky O'Grady aided in understanding how art is placed into books. Professor Linda Walton offered great advice about the Song Dynasty. Our Cleveland State University librarians were tireless in helping me understand copyrights, find publishers, and locate books: Director Glenda Thornton, Gail Marredeth, Barbara Gauthier, and Diane Kolosionek. Pam Eyerdam, art librarian for the Cleveland Public Library, was amazingly helpful with suggestions. Lilianna Gershenovich, a former student from Moscow, wrote permission letters for me in Russian. Monks at the Holy Dormition Byzantine Monastery in Sybertsville, Pennsylvania, were especially kind in allowing me to use their icon here.

General Director Lebedeva of the Tretyakov Gallery of Moscow and her assistant, Marina Ivanova, were so generous in granting permission to use most of the Russian icons in this book—I am so grateful!

Much gratitude goes to Rebecca McClanahan of the Kenyon Writers Workshop and our workshop participants, especially Ellis Morris Prewitt and Sonia Sepic. Their comments were helpful beyond what they could ever know. Also invaluable were the comments from Professor Kathryn C. Lavelle throughout this entire process—always clear and effective. Several of my Cleveland State Writing Center tutors provided excellent feedback and grammatical fixes: Alicia Pavelecky, Stacey Duwe, David Mraz, and Mary Walsh. Emily Troia and Allison Dobbs did a great job in finding images. Former student Maria Wrona took me to a church to view icons, and I thank my former students Michael Crifasi and Amanda McCoy for their understanding of the entire writing process.

A variety of friends have supported me over the years with ideas, listening and the encouragement that I always needed: Penny Riggs, Dan Meltzer, Greg Hayne, David Richardson, Matt Willmann, Tony Bybell, John Leonard, Betty Gump, Doug Stewart, Nilufer Dural, Neda Zawahri, Theresa Nawalaniec, Mary Beth Ions, Gene Lieberman, the inimitable Florence Ions, Isabel and John Tobey, and Sister Carol Kandiko. My family and husband Jim's family have been so supportive: thank you to our parents—William and Pauline Murray and James and Peg McDonald, and to Matt and Ryan McDonald, Bill Murray, Barbara and Michael Turner, Dave Murray, Eileen McDonald, Bill and Diane Hart, Brian and Kathy McDonald, and Danny McDonald and Krista Mousted.

Finally, to the joy of my life, my dear husband, Jim, I give great thanks for all his kindness, patience, and advice.

Introduction

Can meditating with great works of art help you to pray better? Yes, and not only that, you can expect to experience more community, insight, and joy. This joy is what I hope to convey most, as for more than a decade I have seen and keep seeing people of all ages exhausted at their work in all types of employment. My greatest desire in writing this book is to reach out to those who have little time to pray.

This exhaustion might be an aftereffect of what Thomas Merton commented on in *Conjectures of a Guilty Bystander*. Our culture's love of efficiency and misuse of technology creates a "busyness" that Merton considered a type of violence. Add to that a troubled economy where many are out of work and others who do have jobs often do the work of four. How do we counteract these social trends and realities?

There has to be a very fast way of praying, resting in the presence of God, experiencing beauty, making resolutions, and prioritizing. Within these pages is a collection of some of the most poignant and beautiful works of contemplative art on which to begin and form a foundation. The intent of this book is to link the artwork with its spiritual heritage in order to enrich our understanding of the beauty and depth therein.

Christian contemplative artists wish to convey how to apply God's word to daily life and how to rest in God. Chinese contemplative artists from the tenth century hoped to convey the connection between the viewer and the great source of life itself—and all their writings and artwork deliver these messages in ways that we can most quickly use them.

For example:

(1) A brief passage from Thomas Merton can rectify some issues. (2) A glance at an icon can realign priorities instantly. (3) A Chinese landscape painting offers serenity instead of the landscape itself.

While most readers use these contemplative works of art, it will be a treat to understand their composition. The spiritual heritage behind each one is explained here. I chose these three types of contemplative art because each has been written about so much that we can form a secure base from which to draw commonalities. The largest similarities are not hard to guess: each draws on Scripture or sacred texts. Each has the artist creating from contemplative experience. Each rests on monastic spirituality. When these traditions are explored, though, we see monastic values come forth that, if known, can be used more fully. The list below is not exhaustive, but it is a set of values common to all three traditions explored here.

Interactivity: A painting or work of contemplative writing can be said to look back at the viewers, wanting to engage with them.

Communion with God: One of the purposes of Christian contemplative art is to connect viewers with God. The Chinese wanted connection with the life force.

Peace within the self: This art should address neglected issues and summon the best in us.

Connection with community: This art calls us to consider the behavior of others and to seek peace within our communities.

Lessons with nature: Chinese artists of the Song Dynasty especially saw nature as creating the best in us and leading us to contemplation.

Insight: Contemplative art often leads us to dissonance and resolution.

An ordered way of life: Contemplative art leads viewers to seek peace through the law of God or through tranquility within self, home, and society.

An invitation to further contemplation, silence, and serenity: This art encourages the quiet contemplative experience of the artist him- or herself.

Healing: People throughout the centuries have spoken of the healing properties of these art forms.

Protection: Icons protected cities, and Chinese art protected an entire culture.

Why don't most readers know these monastic values, even if they use contemplative art now to pray? Largely because contemplative spirituality can be absent from Catholic schools and parishes, although some groups, such as Contemplative Outreach, do make presentations throughout the country, and some parishes offer contemplative prayer, retreats, or occasional music services.

The need for contemplative values today is very great, which is why so many readers are already familiar with these artworks. One of the reasons why these values are so needed is that the number of decisions people have to make today is staggering, and many times the decisions have a very tight time frame. What to put first—family, the needs of the self, our work responsibilities, our community efforts—can tax us all.

Insight is something monastics seek because they want to understand the word of God, and they want us, who do not have nearly as much time to discern Scripture, to benefit from their efforts. Christian monastics pray the psalms in their entirety each week. This poetry is the basis of their lives, and their artwork in writing or in icons witnesses the struggle that we find in those psalms, models of insight themselves. The artwork found here might be a springboard for readers to begin the practice of monastic reading, called *lectio divina*, to enhance their ability to find God's will in their complicated lives.

Most readers already make wonderful decisions. Yet better ones—ones that yield peace and bring joy, the hallmark of the contemplative life—can be had when we are aligned with our values. The contemplative adds peace in valuing rest. Andre Louf, in his book *The Cistercian Way*, notes that Guerric the abbot of Igny believed that in every type of work we ought to seek rest as did Mary in the story of Mary and Martha in the Gospel. The contemplative under Benedict's Rule never shirked work or community responsibilities. However, the emphasis of rest during labor helps lay contemplatives order their daily lives. Merton condemned the inability to keep to a focused, quiet life in *Conjectures of a Guilty Bystander*. While we don't have the same conditions, we can draw from monastic knowledge and experience, and, most of all, focus on love.

EXPLORING THESE TRADITIONS

One summer I sat researching icons—a stack of books reached my head—and yet, for all this writing on icons, few consider the spirituality behind them. I'm sure this reluctance to discuss the spiritual motivations of artists is due to the academic world's tendency to favor information or facts. One art book, for example, had perspective lines drawn on trace paper over an icon of Mary and Jesus. This hesitance to understand the motivation behind contemplative artwork is also due to the amount of reading a scholar would have to do in spiritual texts that such discussions would require. It is not uncommon in art books to have a sentence appear that states the link of various artworks to a specific religion or to a kind of spirituality, but the real study of both together is rare.

I turned to books that did discuss spiritual sides of art, and this split between the university and the world of artists was mentioned, just as it is when monks discuss the effects of the rise of the university on their reading. Mary Caroline Richards, in her book *Centering in Pottery, Poetry, and the Person,* is especially clear in voicing how much she wanted monastic values within a university structure. She, like monks, values the individual person, insight, vocation, wisdom, the application of knowledge to character, and the holiness of matter. She felt deeply sad that nowhere did university instruction have students applying knowledge to values and character.

Sister Wendy Beckett opened a door for many when she simply responded to art and gave the gift of the ability to respond to so many. In our art appreciation classes, we might have learned about an artist or a style, but not how to respond. Only contemplatives like Richards or Sister Wendy Beckett can offer us that gift because they highlight the experience of art as opposed to learning about art and artists.

Other writers like Sue Bender and Frederick Franck show us how to look and what to see. Standing in front of an Amish quilt in a department store, Bender was captivated by its vivid colors, notably black, and eventually chose to live with an Amish family to understand what it was that drew her so. It was, in large part, their spirituality which embraced, as monks do at vigils, the bleakest sides of life. If Bender shows how powerfully a work of art can draw us, Franck teaches us how to see. Instead of his usual activities of looking, drawing, or taking a photograph, Franck coupled these activities with experiencing the subject of the art. Franck chose to allow it to take up as much space in his own experiencing as possible. He believed that seeing enabled him to respect what he would draw and to paradoxically release or mirror that image in a way that honors its being.

Yet the experience of art itself is not the subject of this book. And neither is contemplation itself. We find that they are so separate, cut off from their spiritual roots, and that's what I would like to pull together here.

Contemplation and meditation are found everywhere today. Many famous people make no secret of their meditation. Wellness centers offer classes in guided imagery; many yoga classes end in meditation; in bookstores, CDs are available with soothing sounds for meditation; and psychologists like Daniel Goleman have worked with the Dalai Lama to bring the powerful effects of contemplation to children in schools. Ours is a culture that needs to find the rest and quiet that contemplation and meditation deliver. Each of the above resources, however, is divorced from its spiritual roots to allow a great number of people to enjoy these resources. This book connects them. It offers readers the spiritual heritage of several well-researched forms of contemplative art in order that they may better appreciate the artworks and use the values behind their composition.

This book shows that the monastic roots of such art are very powerful for community. We don't always see that link when these spiritual roots are cut. This art leads us to participate in the mysteries of our salvation in Christ. It also allows us to be connected with God, ourselves, nature, and others. Concern for such connection is a fruit of contemplation that can sometimes get lost when the peace and rest that contemplation and meditation bring are highlighted. Understanding the roots of this art enhances our ability to practice meditation and contemplation in our daily lives.

The Heritage of *Lectio Divina*

Section I will discuss the heritage of *lectio divina* more fully. To briefly introduce it, *lectio divina*, or sacred reading, refers to particular processes of prayer with readings. The most notable readings are those of sacred Scripture, but other sacred texts can be used as well to foster the application of knowledge, the understanding of various situations, and rest in God. Unlike prayer that asks God for something, a monastic using *lectio divina* receives and ponders what is read. Guigo the Carthusian is credited with describing what are called the four moments of this type of prayer that moves among (1) a literal reading, (2) a reading to apply the reading to oneself, (3) a reading that encompasses community, and (4) one that rests in God. As Thomas Keating describes it, there were never stages of this sort of prayer, even though it might lend itself to that misunderstanding. In short, a monastic uses *lectio divina* to break open Scripture or other sacred texts in order to develop the experience of God within him- or herself.

The contemplative artist steeped in *lectio divina* would most likely place more of an emphasis on a viewer's or reader's using the artwork than would most artists. This is what Thomas Merton did in his writings. He hoped his writing would spur readers to a greater connection with God and a greater ability to choose the good. This book aims to help readers understand and use both the process of *lectio divina* and artwork made with it as its underpinnings.

The Heritage of Icons

Section II will consider the heritage of icons in greater detail. Monks who are iconographers seek to convey monastic values through particular interesting distortions. Haloes that spill over a border speak to holiness that abounds from the figure portrayed. The contrasting colors of inner and outer garments mirror the inner and outer lives. Streamlined noses and ears mean we should close off those senses so we can amplify our inner gazing and our spirit world within. So much is said with the simplest colors: black, our fallen nature; gold, the world of God. While these are the entry points to understanding icons, the spirituality of the icon points to silence as the way to know God. The development of the inner world through the discipline of attention and loving devotion is what iconographers also hoped to inspire.

Russian iconographers, especially those of the twelfth to fourteenth centuries, learned the value of silence, or heyschasm, which refers to the quiet experienced as the way to find God. Catherine De Heuck Doherty wrote very well about this experience in her books *Poustinia* and *Molkanie* (which refers to holy silence). The famous iconographer Andrey Rublev studied under Saint Sergius, who was a great advocate of cultivating silence. Readers new to this form of contemplation might want to turn to Doherty first because she is so readable.

The Heritage of Song Dynasty Landscape Paintings

Section III explores the contemplative culture of the Song Dynasty. Re-markable for their tranquility, Song Dynasty paintings, like icons, offer great lessons in spirituality through similar *distortions*. Nothing is centered, as are most Western paintings. Silent space, often filled with mist, greets the viewer. Sometimes a small figure will appear as if in gratitude in a magnificent scene. Nothing is perfect: lines drawn will not be complete— sometimes brush strokes are very clearly seen as brush strokes. It is only a painting. Color and shading are not emphasized. This art form, though, was believed to offer viewers the calm they needed, especially if they were city dwellers without ready access to nature. Like the iconographer, the Chinese artist hoped to inculcate various spiritual and personal values.

Although this art tradition is not Christian, the entire culture that espoused and fostered such art was contemplative and can teach us much. Imagine everything—government, schools, training—all devoted to contemplation. That's why this tradition is included here.

How to Use This Book

While the first three sections delve into the spiritual heritage behind the three contemplative traditions, the fourth offers readers a chance to practice using the gifts that monastic artists want us to have. It offers questions that point toward various monastic principles that can be applied to readers' daily lives. The reflection questions can be answered right in the book. While readers may find them to be simple questions, they point toward creating peace and love in their lives. The Cistercians have a nickname for themselves, the school of charity, in response to the university culture's school. Espousing their values leads to greater joy and peace in our lives.

A section on further reading offers a variety of ways to continue reading about contemplative spirituality. There are groups of lay contemplatives throughout the country that readers can explore. Readers can find many more icons and Chinese paintings at Wikimedia Commons by searching for Andrey Rublev, Russian icons, and Sung Dynasty ("Song" is the more recently preferred spelling).

It is my hope that readers would use Section IV and the art and Thomas Merton quotations that follow page 42 to address various issues in their own lives with the values that monastic artists hold. Books are recommended as ways to expand our understanding of monastic spirituality, which has at its heart the joy of the focus on Christ.

★

Let's Practice

Our Lady of Vladimir

One way to pray with an icon is to zero in on one feature. Let's pick the star on her shoulder or the face of Jesus. You could also focus on the juxtaposition of the face of Mary next to the face of Jesus. Pick something that you are drawn to. As you look at that image, ask yourself what aspect of spirituality or what spiritual message is depicted.

For instance, the star could refer to her regal status; the face of Jesus can bring up concern he has for Mary; the juxtaposition can highlight the issue of attention—whether we put it on the world or on Christ. Then ask yourself if there is any aspect of your daily life that this spiritual message could inform. Do you need,

for instance, to remember that the queen of heaven is helping you? Do you need to know Christ cares for you? Do you need to understand that your attention needs to be drawn toward Christ?

Spending time meditating on the images in this book will offer you fast messages when you can just glance at them throughout the day.

★

The *Lectio*-Inspired Prose of Thomas Merton

It is the quiet long before dawn breaks, the night sky still dark, and monks at the Abbey of Gethsemani in the 1940s turn from vigils to several hours of silence before the next service, lauds. These hours are considered the holiest time of the day, so some are headed back to their cells to pray in silence, while others remain in church.[1] The hallway they exit church into is dimly lit, without windows, and only shuffles are heard.[2] Once dawn breaks and lauds are finished, some walk to the refectory for chicory-coffee and bread. Thomas Merton, who would have been known by his religious name of Father Louis, might have walked some days to a private place, his vault of old manuscripts in the south corridor near the Abbot's office, the place where he was assigned to do his writing.

He would pull out a very long, gray key to unlock what resembled any other library: the vault's steel had been encased by wallboard, and books on metal shelves lined the room. Vestments were kept there too, so a faint odor of mothballs filled the air.[3] Through the window he could see a dogwood and enjoy the stillness of the earth. Even amid all this silence, though, the psalms that he had heard at vigils often present the harshest emotions, selected to match the peak time of night: betrayal, grief, guilt, and vengeance, to name a few. Merton would have been thirty-two years old, wearing a white cotton twill robe, the black scapular and leather belt, and just beginning to teach men studying to be priests.

It was 1947, and Merton was assigned the daunting task of completing a history of the Cistercian Order, at that time 849 years old. Many rare books and manuscripts filled the room thanks to Dom Edmond Obrecht, who had collected them from monasteries all over the world. Some were thin and worn, others with lovely handwriting, some written in Latin, many in French. They detailed foundations in twenty-two countries, including France (La Trappe, Clairvaux, and more), the newest one in Utah, and the heartbreaking ones from the 1800s in America.

Merton was astonished at how many projects he had going, although the history of the order was the only thing he wanted to write.[4] What captivated him was seeing one particular pattern arise.[5] It paralleled a pattern in his own life, and perhaps this assignment helped cement it: He was six years into his monastic life, settled in, having completed *Seven Storey Mountain*, the autobiography that touched millions with its account of the old Merton who left the world. But what of this new man, the monk? And what of that commitment to an entirely new way of life? Was it worth the risk and sacrifice that the night sky symbolized—a life waiting on God, listening in silence, reading to promote love, and enduring the chosen ascetic hardships?

✱

Having reviewed almost nine centuries' worth of Trappist foundations, Merton saw that only groups of monks who remained unattached to their activities and who placed the commitment to the contemplative vocation above all else lasted. It was so easy, as he often saw in his studies, for a community or individuals to slip into activity for excellent reasons, but these foundations did not last, no matter how valuable the goals. He sorrowed over the intense activity in Kentucky in the early 1800s—monks who diffused their efforts among teaching, traveling, and work—and it all amounted eventually to nothing.[6] He tells of those foundations in other parts of the world whose spirituality was off the mark, not emphasizing contemplation and the protection of God that *The Waters of Siloe*,[7] which he titled this history of Isaiah 8:6, symbolized. He wrote that these foundations failed to attract new members.[8] His own vocation, one he doubted for years, must have felt more secure once he had written this history. The tone of the book, which can only be described as rollicking, must signal that joy.

It is quite significant that Merton makes this connection about the contemplative life in a room surrounded by books and manuscripts because they are a key part of monastic culture, a doorway toward the kind of contemplative life monks knew they needed. The vestments as well signal the role of priest in the order itself and in Merton's life as one of sacrifice leading to salvation.

When considering the writings of Thomas Merton, particularly the contemplative classics that have never gone out of print, we can easily distance ourselves from them by saying they came about through Merton's genius, divine inspiration, or the foresight of Dom Frederic Dunne[9] ordering him to write. Essential to this power of Merton's writing, and often overlooked, is the role of his monastic culture in forming his ideas about reading and writing. As Lawrence S. Cunningham writes in *Thomas Merton and the Monastic Vision*, there is no understanding of Merton without placing him within his culture—one that bases itself on listening through reading. What Merton brought, his poetic eye that saw right to the core of any issue, fit deeply within this culture that so valued connection and application.

Monastic values surrounding reading and writing permeate the more mature works of Merton the monk. They do not permeate his earlier works, even though his genius, wording, and inimitable personality do. In these earlier works—journals like *Run to the Mountain* (1939–1941) and *Entering the Silence* (1941–1952), and an early journal-like novel *My Argument With the Gestapo* (1941)—he is searching, stretching, and playing, but he is not viewing, reading, and writing in the same ways he does once his feet are planted within his order. This change in his writing has great significance. No matter whether a person prefers Merton's writing from the 1950s on contemplation or his later social writing, both have great power, and the role that sacred reading plays in the monastery in shifting his attitude toward text is often ignored.

The spiritual heritage that shapes the contemplative artist is the key to understanding and implementing his or her work of art. In Merton's case, this heritage refers to the active search for God through reading and writing. Reading was never seen as a passive activity for gaining information. We have inherited a sense of reading as informative and a sense of art as inert, and both prevent us from fully reflecting on and applying the messages that contemplative artists long to give.

Ancient Monastic Reading

As far back as fifth-century synagogues, reading was done with particular devotion. The Greek word *proseuchein* referred to such reading.[10] Men would sit listening intently to make moral decisions, to apply the readings, not only to fulfill a requirement.[11] The passage from hearing into action was expected. The early spiritual writer Origen passed this type of reading on to monasticism.[12]

When a Jew from this period or a monk from the fourth to twelfth centuries was reading or listening to a text—scriptural or spiritual—he or she believed that the text was alive and speaking personally to each listener.[13] The text was always viewed in these cultures as interactive. Hearing or reading the text, the reader would then seek to apply the text to his or her own life, and by extension, the life of the community.[14] When Jewish readers and monks were expecting to make moral decisions (*halahka*), there was an implicit belief not only in change as a fundamental aspect of reading, but in the ability of the reader or listener to apply the text to his or her own situation. Duncan Robertson writes in his book *Lectio Divina: The Medieval Experience of Reading* that the monk memorized Scripture in order to own it with heart and mind and body. In owning it, he acted on it in his own individual way, allowing it to manifest in his life.[15]

The place of reading in the community and for individuals was outlined in the writings of Saint Benedict of Nursia (c. 480–547) once monastic communities acquired his small manual for monastic life. It was a holistic activity. When Saint Benedict advised brothers to read privately if they wished "without disturbing the others," he was referring to the practice of reading aloud, which was done so that the reader would slow down and concentrate. Medieval physicians assigned reading as another form of exercise,[16] like they would assign walking or running. The reader was united in mind, body, and spirit while reading.

Reading was given the status of being next after work and feast days, very much integrated with nature, as these were. Like his Jewish predecessors, Benedict put livelihood before reading in order to ensure his monks the quiet they needed to live. Occasions of reading in church or in private were shortened at times of harvest and rearranged again during winter when more time could be spent reading. Feast days, like Easter or Christmas, altered times for reading. However, once these two priorities were met, reading (and its implicit link to the divine and to community) came next. If all this sounds too ideal, it is. Benedict knew of the tendency to shirk reading. For instance, during Lent, when a suggestion of his is to "finish a book," he also advises two senior monks to make rounds to chasten any less diligent readers. [17]

Further contrast to our own culture comes when we see how little attention monks paid to what we value in reading. If we had a text of only eight pages, we would probably consider the thing as a whole. Saint Bernard of Clairvaux believed that a little yielded much in *lectio* because he believed the divine to be hiding, or modest, within the text.[18] In his own writings, he spent thirteen years writing sermons on the very brief Song of Songs, and, while he composed eighty-three of them, he "never got past the third chapter."[19]

Completion was important, as we will see, for scholastics, not monastics. Neither was perfection important: Merton's writings contained so many syntactic errors that the censors of the order sent him handbooks. He claimed he was in a rush to get to print,[20] but he was also in a way following monastic beliefs about the real goals of reading and writing.

What has stayed the same regarding the practice of reading, even to this day, is the amount of time monks read. They read collectively in church and during refectory time; they read alone in their cells; leisure time is spent reading; and the 150 psalms, the heart of their spiritual life, are read and sung throughout every week.

Reading for Change and Insight

What was expected to happen during *lectio divina* was a mixture of literal reading, application, prayer, and contemplation. *Lectio divina*, or sacred reading, comprises four moments:

- literal, *lectio* (knowledge of the author, audience, genre, literal meaning),
- reflective, *meditatio* (application of the text to the reader's life),
- moral/behavioral, *oratio* (use of the text to consider moral issues),
- contemplative, *contemplatio*
  (rest in the text, leading of the text to the divine).

Before the rise of the university culture, this process was cyclic. A reader would move in and out of various levels in no particular order.[21] Of most importance was the experience of allowing a reading to challenge the reader either by the application of the reading or by the shift in attitude that a reader might undergo because of the challenge that a passage presented. Because the challenge was the key issue, a reader did not progress through stages.

The most interesting aspect of this process of reading is that each moment asks for connection. The text is connected to the reader's own life, to the community, to the divine. The reader was meant to grow in respect and love of the divine and others through this often solitary reading experience.

During the four moments, the reader is expected to apply the text to his or her own life, to the life of the community, and to the reader's relationship with God, respectively. Therefore, text to the monastic reader is not inert—it is alive and challenging. As a writer, Merton grew in appreciation of texts as such, and so he created them to be challenging to the audience, asking them to make decisions.[22] This process of prayer through reading and application of the reading takes time to become accustomed to, which is why Merton's writing shifts only after he is immersed and committed in his monastic life. This commitment was deepened when he made his solemn profession in 1947 and when he published *The Waters of Siloe* in 1949.

Merton's Unpublished Lecture Notes on *Lectio Divina*

Notes titled *Lectio Divina* were found filed with another manuscript, a chapter on faith from *Seeds of Contemplation* that was published in 1949, and it is not clear whether the manuscript was simply misfiled or whether this is an accurate date, as there is no date on the manuscript itself.[23] These notes, most likely meant for monks who were studying to become priests and who came from all walks of life, display richly what Merton believed *lectio divina* was meant to accomplish. He tells them his purpose at the beginning:

> One of the most important aspects of our monastic formation, and often one of the most neglected, is the development of our mind and heart by *lectio divina* so that we can enter into the wisdom and knowledge of God. Remember that we have come to the monastery to seek God—and to seek Him in the wholeness of our monastic life. Not only in the Office, in the Mass, not only in penance, but also in meditative reading and in contemplative prayer which spontaneously flows from our contacts with God in His word. We come to the monastery not only to praise God, or to obey God, but also and above all to know God in that knowledge which flows from love and leads to more love. Knowledge and love must go together. They must complete and assist one another, and bring us deep into the mystery of Christ.[24]

Merton refers here to Saint Augustine, who wrote that nothing could be well-known that wasn't loved. Throughout Part 1 of these notes, Merton highlights connection as the vital aspect of reading: reading for the connection with God, for the understanding of one's entire life which was summed up in vocation, and for the connection of the reader to the meaningful parts of the text. Reading, especially but not exclusively *lectio divina*, "must teach us the truth of things as they are, the truth about ourselves, in order that we may conform our lives to this truth, to the reality willed by God, and thus gradually come to know God Himself by union with His will."[25] The best motive for reading was contact with God. Reading, therefore, was *indispensable* for living in God and having God live in us.

Merton gives practical advice regarding beginning to read in general, offering advice on five different subjects. In developing the ability to read, he notes that we have to have motives that lead us to grow spiritually. He warned that simply believing that certain readings are good for us in that they might improve us were not good motives. Only when a strong personal conviction exists to give oneself to God through reading does the motive become a powerful one.

After motive, Merton considers interest. He highlights the individual's development of awareness in order to respond to meaning as he refuses to allow subjectivity to be the entire activity of reading. He notes that a monk's interior life "is only vital and real and valuable when it is a sharing in the common interior life of redeemed mankind—the life of the Church, the mind of Christ."[26] This interior life, he warns, cannot be had from reading diligently only those books that a spiritual director finds valuable.

Once motivation and interest are considered, Merton turns to application. "Nothing will affect us deeply" unless we work to apply these readings. Such application requires awareness of ourselves, "an intelligent use of our faculties, not automatism, not confusion. A free and mature use of our mind and will."[27] Patience and humility are required, too, as we might be tempted to read things beyond our ability, or we might grow discouraged at how difficult it is to enact what we read.

Next, Merton considers method, how we read. Even though *lectio divina* is considered for the monk the highest form of reading, to skip simpler types of reading may prevent a monk from really praying. Here Merton turns to what most readers will readily identify as common advice for reading: pre-reading by placing a book in its context, identifying our purpose in reading, reviewing, and pretending to explain the content to someone else.

Finally, Merton suggests guidance to shape taste and interest. He advised a spiritual director with "breadth of view and discretion, not one who thinks the mind of the Church is confined to a narrow range of pious books which will distort one's outlook instead of forming it, if not balanced by the whole truth of dogma, etc."[28] Conversely, Merton thought that the director could have insight into character and personality, and that the director could select appropriate books for spiritual development. None of this development could occur, however, without the aid of the Holy Spirit, who helps all of the above stages of reading. Merton even devotes a few pages to dryness in prayer and reading, where he advocates forgetting the self and letting go of the need for knowledge. He seems throughout to be a thorough and compassionate guide of the men listening to his lectures. He neither ignores their intelligence nor allows them to skip fundamental aspects of reading.

When Merton shifts to Part 2, his discussion rests on one example, Septuagesima Sunday. Far from simplifying the experience, Merton delves into the greatest mysteries of our faith because Septuagesima Sunday refers to the third Sunday before Lent, when we set our sights on Easter and the preparation needed during Lent—a day when the readings range widely from the sweetness of creation and our fallen nature to the end of the world and God's mercy and salvation. It was removed from the liturgy in 1969.

To engage in *lectio divina*, according to Merton, we have to remember that we are using it to worship God, and the best way to do that is to engage in the liturgy of the Church, as Scripture and liturgy allow us to participate in the mysteries of our salvation, and both are meant for us to adore God:

> The Catholic must, then, be able in some way to read the Bible as his book, as a book, which, though often obscure, disconcerting, and difficult, will often unexpectedly reveal its mysteries to the very depth of his being, so as to change his whole life in its inmost depths and turn him anew to God. How will he do this? By union with the *Ecclesia orans*, the praying Church, as she herself meditates on the Scriptures.[29]

Merton adds, "here in the liturgy they enter into the mystery in participation with Christ Himself, and they grasp the meaning of the sacred texts precisely in their relation to the act which he accomplishes, here and now, in the liturgical mystery!"[30] Merton reiterates throughout these notes that understanding Scripture fully is possible only with the aid of the Holy Spirit.

Merton gives some historical background: The readings arise from "the influence of the Oriental Church, which had moved the beginning of the Lenten fast back to the opening of their liturgical year....The reading of the creation narrative from Genesis springs from this fact."[31] He adds that the profundity of the readings of this Sunday stem from its origins:

> The political situation of the West, ravaged by wave after wave of barbarian invasions, was desperate. Everyone believed the end had come. The sorrow and near-despair of a society pushed to the limit of endurance makes itself felt in this Office. This extrinsic factor was used by the Holy Spirit to give a special fruitfulness to the Church's meditation of Scripture in this Office.[32]

As Merton begins to discuss the various readings, we can see that the monk is privileged to reflect in one day on the greatest mysteries of the Church.

That is, the monk would hear the "beautiful and limpid sentences of Genesis. 'In the beginning God made heaven and the earth...,'" contrasted with the doctrine of original sin from Saint Augustine, followed by reflections on the end of the world in Matthew 20, and then "the necessity of mortification" in order to reach heaven in 1 Corinthians 9—all of which, says Merton, lead to "hope and confidence" that God "can use sin for sanctification if we do penance" and "let Him work in our lives."[33] Merton writes that "The Office brings us an obscure and mysterious participation in the peace of the Risen Savior, living in Heaven and reigning, through His Holy Spirit, in our own hearts."[34]

Lectio divina on this particular Sunday for Merton meant a symphony of readings: his own love of literature shows as he mentions the "juxtapositions" of readings and the cadences and rhythms. He appreciated the beauty and mystery of Scripture, adding in the last segments of these notes some references to *Meditations Before Mass* by Romano Guardini, who argues it would be theoretical and foolish to use only the intellectual content of Scripture and exclude the sound, nature, or effect of the words themselves. The final pages of Merton's notes contain only lines of Scripture, such that his notes move from the most general advice on reading to the most specific attention to Scripture itself.

These notes show the depth of formation in *lectio divina* that Merton had. They also reveal a glimpse of Merton's deep faith and his compassion for men of all walks of life entering into the role of priest, many of whom would be future abbots in countries all over the world. As Father John Eudes Bamberger wrote in *Reflections on the Way of Prayer,* Merton never deviated from this monastic formation, even in his ventures into Eastern traditions. These notes also show how greatly he valued the connection with Christ in the liturgy, with others in the Church, and with the language especially chosen by God in Scripture.

The Loss of the Interactive Reading for Wisdom

Why did Merton's writing change, and what made it so powerful? We can compare passages of writing before Merton entered the Cistercian Order to ones after he is settled, and the difference is that his own texts become interactive and experiential at the levels of connection that only monks would practice. What Merton found was lost to Western culture at the rise of the university in the 1200s: reading for *wisdom*.

By the time of the 1200s, university students did go to monasteries to study, but it was more typical for monks to attend universities.[35] It was there that monks learned the ways of systematic thought that shaped excellent theology but stifled the spontaneity of contemplative prayer.[36] Thus what was once a cyclic experience turned into four stages, which, although fine for learning, never really existed as such.[37] As early as 1134, one monk, Hugh, complained that the *sapientia* [wisdom] of sacred reading was being lost.[38] Today, in their books and articles on *lectio divina*, writers like Michael Casey, Joan Chittister, Christopher Dillon, Thomas Keating, Basil Pennington, and Norvene Vest have helped to restore what was lost even to monks.[39]

These monastic beliefs about the value and the use of reading come out most when passages from Merton's early writing are contrasted with those from when he is firmly a part of his order. In any of Merton's journals, it is not easy to find a short entry where he is reflecting on a text. Below, however, is an entry from *Conjectures of a Guilty Bystander*, a collection of later journals where Merton employs several readily identifiable *lectio* principles. It is unlikely that the average person would read this passage like a monk would and as Merton does, by moving into the behavioral and mystical levels. These levels were the most discarded at the rise of scholasticism and therefore most needed today, for they foster community with others and with the divine. In the following passage, Merton extends his reflection into these realms, with hopes of moving the reader toward a deeper humility and respect for the self:

> Gabriel Marcel says that the artist who labors to produce effects for which he is well known is unfaithful to himself. This may seem obvious enough when it is badly stated: but how differently we act. We are all too ready to believe that the self that we have created out of our more or less inauthentic efforts to be real in the eyes of others is a 'real self.' We even take it for our identity. Fidelity to such a nonidentity is of course infidelity to our real person, which is hidden in mystery. Who will you find that has enough faith and self-respect to attend to this mystery and to begin by accepting himself as unknown? God help the man who thinks he knows all about himself.[40]

A comparable passage occurs in his earliest journal, *Run to the Mountain*, dated December 8, 1939:

Saint Teresa [of Ávila]—*The Interior Castle*—says we must not dwell on self-knowledge alone, but pass on from it at once and go seeking God's love above everything, because every other desire is a traitor and every other knowledge is vain without God. Without the love of God, or the explicit desire for him, self-knowledge is futile and makes one very miserable, because one seeks this way to get out of a blind alley—and never does. We only think we want to know about ourselves, but we really want to know God.

I was so preoccupied with self-knowledge that I didn't know anything about anybody else's feelings.

Tonight I saw some old letters from various people. I wondered how I ever deluded myself that I knew how to read when I had simply not read one third of the things that were said in those letters although I read the words over and over again.[41]

Many of the same elements appear in this passage, as in the first passage, yet the text is more of a report of information than the rich synthesis of the previous one. The early journals are rich in reflection and in Merton's perennial concerns of identity, vocation, society, learning, art, and nature, but they are not filled with the kind of writing that is a product of *lectio*. Once he is practicing monastic values leading toward reading and writing, Merton's connection to others, to himself, and to the divine increase. The weight and mystery of such connections are articulated.

In *Conjectures of a Guilty Bystander*, Merton reflects on a quote from Gandhi:

"'The business of every God-fearing man,' says Gandhi, 'is to dissociate himself from evil in total disregard of the consequences. He must have faith in a good deed producing only a good result....He follows the truth though the following of it may endanger his very life. He knows that it is better to die in the way of God than to live in the way of Satan.'"[42] In Merton's reflection, we see him again move into the realm of the behavioral and mystical moments of *lectio*, helping readers prioritize:

This is precisely the attitude we have lost in the West, because we have lost our fundamentally religious view of reality, of being, and of truth. And that is what Gandhi retained. We have sacrificed the power to apprehend and respect what man is, what truth is, what love is, and have replaced them with a vague confusion of pragmatic notions about what can be done with this or that, what is permissible, what is feasible, how things can be used, irrespective of any definite meaning or finality contained in their very nature, expressing the truth and value of that nature.

We are concerned only with "practicality"—"efficiency": that is, with means, not ends. And therefore we are more and more concerned only with immediate consequences. We are prisoners of every urgency. In this way we so completely lose all perspective and sense of values that we are no longer able to estimate correctly what even the most immediate consequences of our actions may turn out to be. We know well enough that if we do certain things, certain definite reactions will follow: but we lose all capacity to grasp the significance of those reactions, and hence we cannot see further than the next automatic response. Having lost our ability to see life as a whole, we no longer have any relevant context into which our actions are to be fitted, and therefore all our actions become erratic, arbitrary, and insignificant. To the man who concerns himself only with consequences everything soon becomes inconsequential, nothing "follows from" anything else, all is haphazard, futile, and absurd. For it is not humanly possible to live a life without significance and remain healthy. A human life has to have a human meaning, or else it becomes morally corrupt.

Hence we come to be forced to do evil in order to avoid what seem to us evil consequences....But when one chooses to do good irrespective of the consequences, it is a paradox that the consequences will ultimately be good, and the good in them will far outweigh the possible evil.[43]

The practice of *lectio* enabled Merton to reach great truths from his own reflections. When he stated that *we no longer have any relevant context into which our actions are to be fitted*, he was thinking behaviorally, applying Gandhi's words to American society. He extended his knowledge further when he stated the consequences he saw coming from the lack of a relevant context: *all our actions become erratic, arbitrary, and insignificant*. These reflections lead him and readers to the deep respect for God, for the individual, and for the community. They are the hallmarks of *lectio*.

For Merton, it took over six years to fully integrate into his writing the deep levels of application, reflection, and connection that the monastic way of reading taught him. He was probably deeply affected by the process of *lectio divina* because of his earlier love of reading and learning. This way of reading based on love is the focus of the Cistercian Order. Theirs is a school of charity, and, after 900 years, their method of reading still yields that result. Merton wrote in *Is the World a Problem?* "If the deepest ground of my being is love then in that very love itself and nowhere else will I find myself, and the world, and my brother and Christ. It is not a question of either-or but of all-in-one. It is not a matter of exclusivism and 'purity' but of wholeness, wholeheartedness, unity and Meister Eckhart's *Gleichheit* (equality) which finds the same ground of love in everything."[44] The monastic tradition trains us to recognize love in our inmost being. As he wrote in "Problems and Prospects," also in *Contemplation in a World of Action*:

> The charism of the monastic life is the freedom and peace of a wilderness experience, a return to the desert that is also a recovery of (inner) paradise. This is the secret of monastic "renunciation of the world." Not a denunciation, not a denigration, not a precipitous flight, a resentful withdrawal, but a liberation, a kind of permanent "vacation" in the original sense of "emptying." The monk simply discards the useless and tedious baggage of vain concerns and devotes himself henceforth to the one thing really necessary—the one thing that he really wants: the quest for meaning and for love, the quest for his own identity, his secret name promised him by

God (Apocalypse 2:17) and for the peace of Christ which the world cannot give (John 14:27). In other words the monk renounces a life of agitation and confusion for one of order and clarity. But the order and clarity are not of his own making; nor are they, so to speak, an institutional product, an effect of exterior regularity. They are the fruit of the Spirit. The monastic life is a response to the call of the Spirit to espousals and to peace in the wilderness (Hosea 2:19–20)....It is also a charism of brotherhood in the wilderness....It is then a charism of special love and of mutual aid in the attainment of a difficult end, in the living of a hazardous and austere life. The monk is close to his brother insofar as he realizes him to be a fellow pilgrim in the spiritual "desert."[45]

The paradox of *lectio* is that the willed solitude of prayer yields the space and time to prioritize all of the love and connection that comes from its practice.

That this pattern of reading and writing endured throughout Merton's life is clear when we look at a passage written in *Learning to Love*, a journal written in the last years of his life. The following passage is marked by the informality of a journal in that it has many fragments, yet the same pattern from *lectio* is present. In this passage, Merton reflects on writing:

The work of writing can be for me, or very close to, the simple job of being: by creative reflection and awareness to help life itself live in me, to give its esse an existant, or to find place, rather, in esse by action, intelligence and love. For to write is love: it is to inquire and to praise, or to confess, or to appeal. This testimony of love remains necessary. Not to reassure myself that I am ("I write therefore I am"), but simply to pay my debt to life, to the world, to other men. To speak out with an open heart and say what seems to me to have meaning. The bad writing I have done has all been authoritarian, the declarations of musts, and the announcements of punishments. Bad because it implies a lack of love, good in so far as there may have yet been some love in it. The best stuff has been straight confession and witness.[46]

We can watch Merton use the strategies of *lectio* when he begins with the verbal noun *being* and links it to *love*. That word then becomes an activity of giving or service, *to pay my debt to life*, and it extends generally and specifically to *the world* and to *other men*. The activity of writing is pulled into the contemplative framework wherein it becomes the joy that Saint Benedict wrote of when he said that if monks were obedient, that they would run to do their duties with joy. When he offers contrasts with his bad writing, the relationship he sees is one not based on love, but on hierarchy and threat.

The experience of *lectio* had so permeated Merton's life that we see him relating what Saint Benedict hoped for when he discussed his own writing. Merton moved toward love as the ground of his being and was able to act on that love with the gifts God had given him. *Lectio divina* shaped his awareness of love as the ground of being and love as its purpose. It is this awareness of love in these multiple dimensions that we are missing today when we read. It is the contemplative who can give it back to us in writing and in the visual arts.

Molchanie (Christ Pictured as Silence), etching from *The Icon Handbook*
by David Coomler

СПАСЪ БЛАГОЄ МОЛЧАНІЄ.

SECTION II

Icons as Writing the Word

S ilence before God is one of the key points in the oldest book in the Bible, Job. Yet Job reaches this decision after forty-one chapters and does so not because of any argument presented by his friends, but because he has experienced God firsthand: "I had heard of you by word of mouth, but now my eye has seen you."[47] The *experience* of God was direct and visual, and it permanently changed his view of himself and his actions, leading him to renounce his former arguments against God and to "repent in dust and ashes." God entered a dialogue with Job; through the icon, we hope to be this close to God as well.

This experience of God is what iconographers aim at when they create or write an icon. Yet without an appreciation of this goal, many viewers can feel drawn to icons without necessarily participating as they could. At age eighteen, Thomas Merton himself had such an experience. On vacation in Rome after school, he found himself "fascinated by Byzantine mosaics. [He] began to haunt the churches where they were to be found. . . . unconsciously and unintentionally visiting all the great shrines of Rome."[48] Something far beyond the average experience of looking at art happened to Merton at that time: he even contrasts the experience with icons to other types of church art and relics that, although great, never moved him. The icons alone opened up a world to Merton, such that he filled five pages of his autobiography solely on their impact:

> And now for the first time in my life I began to find out something of Who this Person was that men called Christ. It was obscure, but it was a true knowledge of Him, and in some sense, truer than I knew and truer than I would admit. But it was in Rome that my conception of Christ was formed.[49]

Not only this profound spiritual experience, but further profound experiences followed, much like those of Job. Job recognizes with pain his own arguments as false, and he is blessed with a family at the end of his experience. Merton too is able to reflect on himself and feels reunited with his deceased father:

I was in my room. It was night. The light was on. Suddenly it seemed that Father, who had now been dead more than a year, was there with me. The sense of his presence was as vivid and as real and as startling as if he had touched my arm or spoken to me. The whole thing passed in a flash, but in that flash, instantly, I was overwhelmed with a sudden and profound insight into the misery and corruption of my own soul, and I was pierced deeply with a light that made me realize something of the condition I was in....I think for the first time in my life I really began to pray....[50]

The consequences of such a direct, spiritual experience of God through icons led to profound knowledge and to connections with God, his own soul, and his father. Icons had the same effect as *lectio divina* because they have the same principles of composition.

What is fascinating is that Merton had no knowledge at the time of these principles, even though he was so very well-read in art and literature. Merton's biographer, Michael Mott, wrote that whatever Merton had experienced in Byzantine icons, he had had no way of describing it and no way of understanding why it led him to the intense experiences of prayer that it did.[51] Mott, who is a great artist himself in presenting Merton's biography, focuses on the inchoate inner world of Merton at age eighteen—his depiction creates much sympathy for a young orphan who was brilliant and lacked any direction. The depth of Merton's experience, his references to the place of icons in his life, and how iconography related to his own development as a monk are well articulated by artist and art scholar Donna Kristoff.[52] What is considered here is simpler than the rich depiction and reflection of Mott and Kristoff. An icon is composed to have an effect, yet how is it composed that it does so? Let us look at these effects as Merton described them in his autobiography.

The Doctrine of the Incarnation
"implicit in every line"

At their most basic level, icons present us with startling images, but they are so subtle that the viewer without knowledge of them feels drawn, or senses their spiritual message, but does not linger over the linear aspects.[53] The *Angel Gabriel* has many such interesting but not overwhelming lines (see page A1).

Haloes frequently spill over the edge of the border, indicating expansive holiness. Overly large eyes, bespeaking a quiet, interior vision, ask the viewer to switch to what Henri Nouwen described as an internal commitment to God through adoring with the inner eye.[54] The angel gazes interiorly with love. And, if the soul is meant to look at God, then all the other senses are to be stilled. We see the ears small, the noses streamlined. The other world is to be limited while the inner world is to be devoted to God. The head is enlarged to show reflection and contemplation. The neck too is broad, a symbol of breath or spirit.

Colors also are symbolic: the inner robe is a different color than the outer robe, signaling the great difference between the inner and outer life. Gold and black complement each other referring respectively to the radiance of divine life and our fallen nature. A hand pointing in an icon usually indicates a direction for the viewer to take. The hand of the Child Jesus often pulls Mary's face away from the world and toward himself. Many saints' hands point to Scripture.

Often a strange building sits in an icon (pages A8, A9). Buildings are, as John Baggley writes, "dreamlike" and "are not confined to a precise historical moment of time and space...they belong to the world of spirit, to a world of human consciousness that is richer and more mysterious than the ordinary everyday world of rational decisions and logical activities."[55] Perhaps they symbolize the kingdom of God or the mansions in heaven Jesus spoke of.

Each of these mild distortions points to the particular spirituality of silence and contemplation that treasures the incarnation. The distortions offer a spiritual code for silence and adoration. Further, it isn't only that the icon reminds people to be silent or reminds them of sacred mysteries. These icons serve to manifest the value of matter. Hence their gold and their great beauty also signal to viewers that Christ is present and risen, and that we must seek the kingdom within.

"Full of spirit and vitality and earnestness and power"

Technical merit is of lesser importance to the artist and viewer. What matters most is that special connections be made. When Merton felt overwhelmed by the power of these icons, he was most likely responding to their levels of connection. The icon is said to look back at the viewer, connecting the viewer with the divine. Icons are to be written (not painted) from the contemplative experience of the painter, so the icon is a product of the connection between the painter and the divine. All life is considered sacred because the sacred is present in the icon and in all matter.

The story of the first icon holds the reasons for the connections. Legend has it that King Abgar of Edessa (near today's Syrian border of Turkey) sent a messenger to Christ, and Christ pressed his face into a cloth and gave it to the messenger for the king. That first iconic image said to have been made without human hands became for the Byzantines and Russians the beginning of seeing icons as inspired.

Eight hundred years of war over the nature of icons and their place in worship attests to their power. In the end, they are to be *venerated*, not worshiped. The Russian Orthodox Church commemorates this triumph in a prayer called a *Kontakion* for the First Great Sunday of Lent that is said while icons are held up during a procession:

No one could describe the Word of the Father;
but when He took flesh from you, O Theotokos, He accepted
to be described, and restored the fallen image to its
former beauty. We confess and proclaim our salvation
in word and images.[56]

The icon points to the glory of the incarnation without being worshiped itself.

Many writers agree that icons created after the seventeenth century frequently lack the incarnational or spiritual quality of earlier icons. According to Jaroslav Pelikan, these aesthetics rest largely on belief in the incarnation of Christ; as such, icons model the presence of divine matter.[57] Western influence shifted iconographers' focus toward the actual depiction of the scene with technical perfection. Peter the Great as well as the sixteenth-century illustrated Western edition of the Bible were influential in shifting thought processes in the West.

As Baggley wrote, "Russian devotees of Western art had lost touch with the inner life of their own sacred tradition and the purpose that lay behind the painting of icons."[58] Technical merit became more important than spiritual content, and the artwork truly suffered. The two icons of the *Dormition* display this contrast (pages A10 and A12): They are both beautiful icons used for prayer, yet the one where Christ has a more solemn face—a thirteenth-century Russian icon—is less technically perfect than the one from the twentieth century that could be considered more beautiful. The stern face of Christ asks where the apostles' faith is and thereby involves the viewer more, and the lack of technical merit gives the spiritual message more attention. The later icon still presents the compelling image of Christ holding Mary's soul, but it is far closer to art than we are used to seeing everywhere around us.

Egon Sendler posed a poignant question when he asked why such a spiritual form of art could not withstand the force of rationalism.[59] Rationalism was not the only influence. Leonid Ouspensky wrote that individuality had become cult-like, severing the connections so treasured by iconographers and their communities that led to the shift in painting.

God is experienced for the iconographer and the monastic. Knowing God by not knowing, or what is termed the *via negativa*, allows monks to respect God as entirely different from ourselves. No terms are adequate to describe God. While the set of Thomistic causes or descriptors would be studied and loved, monks still live their lives in hope of finding God personally. This experience of God is also often wordless. The experiences of silence, solitude, and contemplation are the groundwork of how iconographers understand the divine. When these ways of knowing were eschewed by Western culture, the icon lessened in spiritual poignancy.

John Stuart wrote that Byzantine consciousness sought always to understand the essence of things and to grasp this essence as well as possible.[60] All the more of an enigma that icons did not weather change well. When icons are born of the experience of the divine, they are largely, he writes, a way to express ideas that are intangible, beautiful, and unknown.[61] It is ironic and sad that a culture devoted to rationalism would spurn the experience of a contemplative, but that is what happened as seen in the last chapter, when the university culture overrode the monastic way of reading for wisdom. Also overridden was the aspect of community life. Monks were supported in their experiences of contemplation. Icons were an expression of an individual experience that was sought and developed by all in the group.

When connections between the divine and the iconographer are valued by the group, it stands to reason that technical merit is really tertiary. No one expected icons to be perfect if they were relating ideas and experiences. Rather, their imperfections spoke to the quality of human life. And in the Chinese Song Dynasty paintings we will see in the next chapter, imperfections were a specific means of demonstrating the humanity of the painter. In icons, the exaggerated eyes and necks, the simple buildings, the extensions of lines over borders all are messages for viewers to see things Biblically.[62] Baggley wrote that distortions are "used in a consistent way to represent the dematerialized, spiritual form of the subject transfigured by divine grace."[63] Let us now turn to the world of silence and rest that iconographers practiced.

"Its solemnity was made all the more astounding by its simplicity."

Icons arise from silence and point to silence. In the Byzantine and Russian cultures from which icons come, silence is understood as rest in the divine or as inner stillness. Silence as rest in the divine implies a simplicity of one's spirit absorbed as a drop of water into the ocean. Silence as inner stillness is an active state where the interior sense is guarded from distracting thoughts and feelings. Relationships are honored first in these states of silence: relationships with the divine first, and within one's self as keeping quiet.

In this divine silence, the monk finds the deep connectedness to all others and all life. The purpose of icons, wrote Sendler, is to connect with God, which is what we were born to do, to be. Consider in the book of Genesis where Adam and Eve walk with God in the Garden of Eden. This intimate walk with God mirrors what the contemplative iconographer wishes to establish in an icon.[64] Conversely, the silence advocated by the icon also points to the interior and exterior battles Christians face. The particular image chosen often gives suggestions about how to win those battles. Regard how in so many icons either Christ or the Word is pointed to by the figure.

The spirituality of icons, known as hesychasm (stillness, inner tranquility), is found in the book *The Philokalia*, which is a collection of sayings from the Desert Fathers beginning between the fourth and fifth centuries and continuing to the fifteenth century. These sayings were preserved within the monasteries of Mount Athos in Greece for the future use of monks, and as such, they are direct, informative writings on the spiritual life of the monk. As Baggley describes it, hesychasm addresses "the whole being": the intellect as the soul's capacity to know God or truth and the heart which is the "spiritual center of our being."[65] The whole being attempts "union with God in stillness, prayer, dispassion, faith, hope and love" according to Saint John Climacus.[66] Most compelling for the study of icons is that "this type of prayer is linked to the flowering of iconography."[67]

The collection of writings known as *The Philokalia*, which is Greek for *the love of the good*, are the underpinnings of the monastic spirituality of iconographers. In it monks learned from fellow monks how to attain stillness of heart. Sometimes this state of heart comes without effort, and sometimes, as Richard Temple writes, it is "a highly active one maintained by all the powers of attention and spiritual vigilance."[68] In *The Philokalia* monks learn that their inner state of sobriety is going to be assailed by their own natures, by trials, and by demons. Keeping watch over one's own inner state is the essence of *The Philokalia*, and monks who learn to discern their spiritual experiences are rewarded with a tranquility that allows contemplation to go on throughout their days, also referred to as recollection. There is even an icon, *Molchanie* (page 20), that refers to the depth of the silence that a monk experiences and that Russians hold dear.

Let us consider only one passage from *The Philokalia* to see how it warns about attentiveness to the interior state. The writer cautions monks about focusing on being virtuous at the expense of not looking at the battles that take place in the intellect. Their highly valued interior silence could be attacked by demons without the monks' even knowing it. Consider, for example, what Saint Paul wrote in his letter to the Ephesians "our struggle is not against enemies of blood and flesh, but against the rulers, against the authorities, against the cosmic powers of this present darkness, against the spiritual forces of evil in the heavenly places" (Ephesians 6:12). The writer of *The Philokalia* argues that he meant we had to be on guard against attacks and realize that these battles would go unseen by anyone but God and the soul. Without the willingness to monitor one's interior state, such monks, the writer argues, may never experience purity of heart or even be aware of their interior passion.[69]

The only way to address such inner turmoil is to watch one's own thoughts, to be an observer of one's own behavior through meditation and through the desire to know oneself thoroughly. This faculty of watchfulness is called *nipsis* and is considered the prime way to deal with a frazzled state of mind. As Temple writes:

> The main work of the hesychast is to acquire the blessing of attention. For this he must summon what natural gifts he has and develop them so that they serve his spiritual aim. In their undeveloped state they can only serve outer life. But for a higher aim, the intellect,

the heart, and all the physical functioning must be tuned so finely that they work to their fullest capacity. Only then will they be fit for the role they were designed for: the preparation of a place within, where God may enter.[70]

Most people who view icons do not realize the depth of the interior silence that the iconographer had to cultivate in order to paint. Iconographers, especially of early Russia, were well acquainted with *The Philokalia*. When we are affected by an icon, we perhaps experience the incredible development of the monk. It is just this interior development that people so need as they are so very busy. Merton frequently wrote about how damaging it was to the psyche to be overly busy—he considered it a form of violence.[71] The natural draw we feel toward the icon might be an interior sense that more silence and devotion is needed. Even during a busy day, glancing at an icon can help us regain some of that silence.

What many consider the most beautiful icon of all time, *The Holy Trinity* icon by Andrey Rublev, comes during the time period of the greatest cultivation of interior silence. Rublev (1370–1430) lived in the Holy Trinity Monastery at Zagorsk in northern Russia in the middle of the fourteenth century. Saint Sergius (1314–1392), the abbot, was renowned for embodying the ideal of hesychasm. His belief was that any chaos, within or without, could be conquered by silence.[72] His vocation to silence and to the founding of the monastery is widely believed to be the genesis of the greatest icons in Russia, those of Andrey Rublev, and other famous icons.

Konrad Onasch best describes how the spirituality of hesychasm from Saint Sergius entered Rublev's work. He writes that Saint Sergius created an environment of self-imposed discipline, spiritual study, and monastic devotion that allowed Andrey Rublev to apprehend the incarnation of Christ as he experienced the Orthodox liturgy and read the Church Fathers and the lives of the saints. Onasch believed Rublev's icons united his artistic decisions and lived monastic spirituality in the simple forms that icons present.[73] Merton grasped all of what Onasch mentions—the simplicity, the profundity, and implicitly the spiritual learning and discipline—when he saw the icon at Saints Cosmas and Damian Church. He noted that "its solemnity was made all the more astounding by its simplicity,"[74] indicating that unlike all the Western literature he was reading, this art spoke of an interior cultivated garden of the iconographer who ultimately rested in God.

"Christ Himself, present in those churches"

How did Merton know that Christ himself was present in those churches? Since icons are made out of a deep respect of all matter, and when all matter derives from and exists in Christ, then the icon communicates its divine origins. It is our Western culture that splits the sacred from the secular, and in so doing, we remove objects from their sacred nature. Our highways are strewn with litter; our schools with discarded ballpoint pens; our mailboxes with junk mail; our inboxes with spam. Icons, conversely, pronounce how sacred all matter and all nature are. Egon Sendler puts it best in his book *The Icon: Image of the Invisible*:

> In fact, the icon is first and foremost the living proclamation of the value of matter. Being a creation of God, it can bear witness to God. Just by its existence, each icon makes reference to the incarnation. Not in theory, but in practice, the icon affirms that man has the possibility of speaking about God and that he has a language for witnessing to his faith.[75]

Furthermore, an iconographer is writing the Word, not merely drawing images to represent something. As John Stuart wrote in his book *Ikons*, Byzantine artists did not focus their efforts on reproducing an image. Instead, these artists would paint about life itself in that as abstract artists, they created with and within the source of life—they did not stand outside it and render what they saw.[76] Another draw we feel toward icons might be their call to us that life itself, all of it, all matter, is valuable and holy. When we see writing and art as alive and relating to us, we grasp what iconographers wanted to convey.

"True knowledge of Him, in some sense truer than I knew and truer than I could admit."

The real duty and privilege of everyone, according to contemplatives of the Eastern Church, is to walk with God in contemplation, as did Adam and Eve in the Garden. Leonid Ouspensky writes in *The Theology of the Icon* that "the icon does not represent the divinity. Rather, it indicates man's participation in the divine life."[77] Not only did Merton sense Christ's presence, he acknowledges that he learned more about Christ. He did so because he shifted from knowledge about someone to participation in that divine life to which he was called.

Participation in the divine life needs to be seen with intuition, says Baggley.[78] The icon speaks to the inner world while reminding us of the sacredness of the natural world. It is also the world of experience that is being addressed (which is a preferred mode of knowing for the monastic community). As Baggley writes of the non-naturalistic buildings that appear in icons,

> The wider significance of the events portrayed has to be worked out in the soul of those who behold the icon;...its fuller significance is found in the inner world where the true work of purification, illumination, and union have to be accomplished. Thus the non-realistic buildings...can open up to us the awareness that it is our own inner world that is being addressed, and to which our attention is being directed.[79]

He continued to say that the beauty of the icon "is linked to a sense of integration and an inner harmony that inspires, attracts, and transforms."[80] Merton's inner world was being addressed and invited to participate in knowledge of Christ that was experiential rather than simply cognitive or informative. This experience lasted Merton's entire life, and he referred to this experience many times throughout his writings.

The contemplative artist shows us in writing or artwork that there is so much more to our spiritual life than simply acknowledging sinfulness and our need for redemption: held equally in writings by Merton and the artwork of iconographers is the richness of peace and communion that exist when our true relationship with God is sought and found.

The Silent Artist

Merton may have seen in icons, obliquely, his own life and his own role as a writer. The training, the spiritual formation, the fasting, and most importantly the contemplative experience of the iconographer are aspects that no one would see when looking at an icon, but they would be totally essential to an icon's composition. The monastic world puts such emphasis on the individual soul, and the icon, as a product of this culture, requires incredible training and respect from the iconographer, but also exists without any acknowledgment of that individual artist. As Baggley wrote, "Beauty, glory, co-operation with the divine energies and sharing in the divine life—these form part of the setting within which icon painters do their work. The icons are created in this environment of faith and worship, and it is to that same environment that they make their particular contribution."[81]

Monks practiced *lectio divina* to know and love God and others through Scripture, but they were also trained in their own monastic heritage that included the ascetic disciplines of fasting, silence, poverty, chastity, and obedience. Every monastic tradition also concentrates on the transformation of character. Spiritual matter is meant to be applied to one's own life, whether it is heard in church or in private. Therefore, iconographers not only had to understand monastic tradition and liturgy, they had to be serious practitioners—there had to be the attempted unity of exterior and interior worlds, the beauty of integration that the Byzantines and Russians so love. The role of Christ as the only hope of achieving such a feat is paramount.

The monk who was an iconographer was not only supported and valued for his or her work, he or she was chosen to write an icon and had to fast for a month before the work was begun. Another person selected the type of icon to be painted, so the monk was told what to paint.

David Coomler, in his book *The Icon Handbook*, writes of how icons were made. Not many manuals survive. The icon itself was painted (in early days) on a piece of wood that was roughened. Gesso (glue from either rabbit skin or fish) was then applied. This glue served to hold several pieces of cloth that became the canvas.[82] Sometimes the gesso was mixed with alabaster or powdered chalk and then polished. When the gesso was dry, which took some time, paints could be applied. Paint was formed from egg yolks and natural colors powdered in (such as cinnabar). Oil mixed with resin (called olifa) protected the surface, but unfortunately collected dust and darkened bright colors.[83]

The drawings themselves were taken from books or manuals (such as the line illustration icons seen in Coomler's handbook). Iconographers would make a stencil by painting with garlic juice on top of the picture in the manual and then putting a piece of paper over this outline. Then they would prick pinholes in this paper, position it over the prepared wooden panel, and lightly dust powdered charcoal over the stencil to form an outline.[84]

Years of apprenticeship went into the skill of painting. Andrey Rublev was apprenticed to Theophanes, whose influence is clearly seen in Rublev's work.[85]

"THE OBSCURITY OF THE PLACE WHERE IT LAY HID, AND ITS SUBSERVIENCE TO HIGHER ENDS"

In relation to the great city of Rome, the church where Merton found the icon was obscure. It wasn't in a gallery of a famous museum, it was in a church where only Catholics went. To Merton, a convert to Catholicism later in his life, that meant this great work of art was wasted. He sensed also that this work of art had much more to do than the works of literature he was reading or than other famous works of art.

Icons are not put on walls for display. Rather, they are used in every aspect of society. They protected cities, they guarded at rituals, they steered individuals. As Baggley wrote, "Church buildings, Imperial palaces, and peasant houses—these are all equally part of the environment of icons; and icons form part of the environment in which monastic spiritual masters, Byzantine and Roman emperors, Greek and Roman peasants and many other Orthodox Christians fulfill their spiritual vocation according to their perception of the Orthodox way."[86]

The wall of icons between the sanctuary and the people, called the iconostasis, serves as a gateway between the world we can see and the world icons point to. Icons hold a special place in Byzantine liturgy because they embody what the liturgy demonstrates: participation in the divine life. We are moved, wrote Philip Sherrard in *The Sacred in Life and Art*, when viewing icons toward archetypal realities of liturgical time and sacred history.

In a home, an icon is displayed on a table with a candle in what are referred to as "beautiful corners." A visitor venerates the icon when entering. When blessed, icons are considered to have power and protection.[87]

There is no question that Merton's experience at age eighteen with an icon was life-changing. This experience, however, can be better understood and even emulated when the composition of icons and their spiritual heritage is known. In the next section, we will consider another form of contemplative art, that of Song Dynasty paintings. These great works of art were designed to help viewers develop their character, connect with nature, order their priorities, and grow in inner silence. They also have a powerful contemplative heritage from which they draw. Like icons, the works of the Song Dynasty painters were deeply treasured by their community. Understanding their composition will again help us better appreciate and use this kind of art.

SECTION III

A World in
a Drop of Ink

Sometime in the T'ang Dynasty (581–907), an ink maker, Xi Tinggui, transported his family over one hundred miles, from Hang Zhou near Shanghai to Huangshan—all for pine trees. Their rich, oily sap, mixed with glue, was what was used to make ink. At the time of Xi Tinggui, however, the ink was so inferior that many paintings and calligraphies faded, and the ones that did last were made with inksticks that had to be aged for forty years.[88] The ink was not permanent, consistent, or defined. Wagering his entire future that the thousand-year-old pine trees in the mountains of Huangshan would yield the richest possible sap, Xi Tinggui set his heart on improving the quality of ink. Legend has it that while his wife was ill, he was mixing a potion for her and found in the root E Gao the perfect glue to accompany the sap, and the ink that has allowed us to see the paintings from that time forward came into being.[89]

What is even more marvelous about this discovery is the award Xi Tinggui received. He was not simply given fame or fortune: he was also given the imperial family name. Emperor Li Yu acquired two of his inksticks and was so overjoyed at the two carp he painted that he changed the ink maker's last name from Xi to Li and established a special branch office of "*mo*" (the character "black" with "soil" on the bottom) that Li Tinggui oversaw.[90] Painting, poetry, and calligraphy—in this dynasty and the next—mattered deeply, as much to royalty as to the entire culture, for many different reasons. Chinese art scholar Sherman E. Lee refers to art critic Ch'en Yu-i, who said that in Buddhist scriptures it is written that even the smallest amount of ink, a single drop, housed a world and all of time that would be present to the heart.[91] The humble ink maker recognized this possibility as much as the emperor.

When the Catholic viewer who wants to augment his or her sense of the contemplative life approaches these worlds of ink, this richness of an entire culture that espoused contemplation will come forth. As Saint Paul advised, "Whatever is honorable, whatever is just, whatever is pure, whatever is lovely, whatever is gracious, if there is any excellence and if there is anything worthy of praise, think about these things."[92] Thomas Merton translated a great Chinese classic, *The Way of Chuang Tzu*, and acknowledged in another book on Asian spirituality the encouragement from Vatican II; namely that there are good spiritual and moral practices to be found in Asian religions that ought to be preserved despite how strained the understanding of these religions are for Catholics.[93] The art of the Song Dynasty will be discussed using monastic terms, for these terms fit the period well and do not, I believe, distort what the Chinese were attempting to do in their art. The ordering of one's life (and thereby the life of the community) through the practice of contemplation is what is common to contemplatives discussed here. Contemplation for the Song Dynasty painters and viewers was never separate from morality, much as it is never separate for practitioners of *lectio divina*.

LANDSCAPE AS SACRED

In their simplicity, the landscapes depicted by Song Dynasty painters synthesize the complicated interaction of the three religious or philosophical traditions converging at this time: Buddhism, Confucianism, and Taoism. The first thing that most people react to when viewing such a painting is the silence of a scene, like the silence in the paintings of water and mountains. Yet this silence is a function of space. As Linda Walton writes, painters understood place as a "repository of the Way."[94] That is, the respect for the Tao, the great life force, was created when a landscape presented space to a viewer, not a representation of a particular place or an imaginative rendering of a fantasy place. Another look at space can be seen in the famous painting "Orchids" by Ma Lin. Space is the primary element of this painting, not the orchids, as lovely and poetic as they are. James Cahill writes that this pre-eminent aspect is considered by painters a specific part of the painting and is present in all three religious and philosophical heritages: the Taoist emptiness, the New Confucian *Ch'i*, and the Buddhist *sunyata*.[95] The subtlety of the space, its expansiveness in landscape paintings, is the silent pointing of the painter toward the Tao, the Way.

Even so, in tension with this ineffable life force is the ephemeral nature of the scene: one knows it is transient, a moment in time when the mist and the light have impressed the poet-painter. It is a scene our imaginations grasp as poetic and eternal, but our intellects know as transient. This aspect points toward the Buddhist influence concerning the transience of things. Max Loehr is especially helpful in describing this aspect of these paintings.

Loehr writes that the world of the Song Dynasty painter is an idealized one where the painter contemplates, free from the mundane concerns of everyday life. Focusing on his own existence, the painter creates a landscape where this same experience is paralleled—empty space, rather than solid forms fill the picture. Highlighting the present moment, atmosphere in the painting takes on an important role. Great attention is paid to atmosphere such that it changes the timelessness of earlier nature painting to the impermanence and transitoriness of a particular moment, deeply felt in these paintings. This shift from an eternal sense of nature to a transitory one allowed viewers a moment away from daily life to briefly but powerfully experience a contemplative moment in time. Subtle expressions of such contemplative moments come in depictions of gathering mist, quiet moments of workers returning home, winds on a lake, or the presence of clouds and mist against huge banks of mountains.[96]

A small scholar figure often appears in these landscapes, solitary or with a student standing a few steps away. Both are engaged in contemplation of the landscape, as in *Viewing Plum Blossoms by Moonlight* by Ma Yuan. The scholars sit or stand off to the side, and their very diminution next to the scene implies their status as hermits and scholars. Confucian doctrines also are apparent in these landscape paintings when the presence of the scholar-poet reminds us of the need for solitude and contemplation.

Not only was nature loved by people of all three religious and philosophical traditions, it was also sought after for other important reasons: Nicole Vandier-Nicolas cites Guo Xi, an important writer of the eleventh century, as saying that landscape offered the development of the mind and inner nature.[97] The viewer gained *xinjiang*, or "the inventive faculty activated by the peaceful contemplation of a landscape" that was "important to convey the authentic flavor of things."[98] Further, in a study of inscriptions at Song Dynasty academies, Linda Walton writes, "The idea that *ch'i* [vital force] accumulated in the mountains and rivers of beautiful landscapes and produced talented men appears with significant frequency in Southern Song early inscriptions."[99] The *ch'i* "produced talented men who transformed landscape."[100] They transformed it because an interior understanding of landscape meant "understanding of universal principle (*li*)," according to academy founder Chu Hsi, as quoted by Walton.[101] *Li* also referred to ordering of both the inner world and of society. As Wucius Wong expressed, when a painter or anyone viewed nature, the emphasis was not on seeing nature during a specific time or a particular place. Rather, that person was believed to be one with nature. The Chinese characters for the word nature are *tsu jen* or self-being, indicating that all of nature rests within us, able to be communicated, and rich with insight.[102]

That these three great religious and philosophical traditions co-existed and are represented in landscape paintings is something that is understudied and under-appreciated. Today when we glance at these paintings, we often feel the contemplation and silence they are meant to offer. Yet we do not realize the depth of the call for viewers, and even for the painter that comes from this rich spiritual heritage. Icons as well ask the viewer and the painter to engage in silence and contemplation.

ACADEMIES AS NURTURING THE CONTEMPLATIVE LIFE

One of the most important aspects of the convergence of the three religious or philosophical traditions is that virtue no longer was a goal, which it was for Confucian scholars: It was a way of life and was taught as such in academies throughout the Southern Song Dynasty and for centuries after. In his translation of the famous Chinese text *The Way of Chuang Tzu*, Thomas Merton wrote that Chuang Tzu criticized Confucian thinking that made virtue a goal. Virtue had to come from within, from the experience of "the mysterious Tao" in contemplation.[103] Once a person was in harmony with the Tao and nature, he or she would act perfectly, called *wu wei* or non-doing, which meant action with respect for the great life principle and oneself and others. Merton saw this act of contemplation akin to what Saint Benedict considered "vital humility."[104]

The painter of the Song Dynasty would be enveloped in an environment where the contemplative vocation was nourished before and beyond the artwork. He (men went to school, not women) would have walked past a shrine on the way to class—a local deity figure would have reminded him of the holiness of that particular site of the academy;[105] an inscription on the walls of the academy would have reinforced the values of virtue, learning, and collegiality;[106] and a garden or a beautiful landscape would have calmed the student on the way to class, even though the academy would be located near a city.[107] Once in class, a grounding in what we would easily term monastic values took place. Painting was not the center of his education, as writing was not the center of Thomas Merton's monastic vocation. He would have spent a great deal of time reading *The Four Books: Confucian Analects, The Great Learning, The Doctrine of the Mean,* and *The Works of Mencius.* Echoes of *lectio divina* can be heard in the following passages from *The Great Learning*:

> The ancients who wished to illustrate illustrious virtue throughout the kingdom, first ordered well their own states. Wishing to order well their states, they first regulated their families. Wishing to regulate their families, they first cultivated their persons. Wishing to cultivate their persons, they first rectified their hearts. Wishing to rectify their hearts, they first sought to be sincere in their thoughts. Wishing to be sincere in their thoughts, they first extended to the utmost their knowledge. Such extension of knowledge lay in the investigation of things.[108]

He would also have spent time reading Chinese Ch'an Buddhist masters who were the most successful of all Buddhist schools at adapting their message to "indigenous currents of thought which had their source in Chinese Taoism."[109] Osvald Siren writes that some Ch'an masters integrated their ideas so much that one expressed "Buddha is Tao, Tao is *dhyana (ch'an)*."[110] Students were encouraged to still their minds "by proper work, life and meditation."[111] When the mind was clear, the artist became "the thing he visualizes or conceives, and if he possesses the proper means of exteriorization, he will transmit in symbols of shapes or signs something which contains a spark of that eternal stream of life or consciousness which abides when forms decay."[112] Siren also writes that for Ch'an students, life was not romantic or easy. Their schools were ones that were strict and very clean to reinforce their values placed on development of "character and self-reliance."[113]

Even so, we are looking at a particular time in history when these conditions existed. A dynasty earlier or later would have found the painter in entirely different circumstances. During the T'ang Dynasty, court scholarship was the center of education, and only men from elite families attended academies, according to Peter Bol.[114] Once the Song Dynasty ends with the Mongol invasion, we find art students as hermits, treasuring their contemplative lives alone.[115] This contemplative stance that flourished during the Song Dynasty in academies produced outstanding artwork that also preserved what is termed the *shih* (or literati) culture. The Mongols did invade, conquering all of China by 1279 and removing all the literati from government, but these Mongols revered the literati culture—so much so that they sought teaching by the Chinese in the "cultural idiom of Confucian rulership," according to Maxwell K. Hearn.[116] The shift that academies made—from vocational schools to prepare men for government service to schools that fostered self-cultivation and sagacity without concern for employment—lasted for centuries beyond the Song.[117] What is more, the artwork that we so treasure today is a lasting remnant of this system of education.

The Head of the Archangel Gabriel, 12th century, RUSSIAN STATE MUSEUM. PHOTO FROM ART RESOURCE, NEW YORK.

THE ART OF CONTEMPLATION

A1

IT DRAWS ME
A2

"If you regard contemplation principally as a means of escape from the miseries of human life, as a withdrawal from the anguish and the suffering of this struggle for reunion with other men in the charity of Christ, you do not know what contemplation is and you will never find God in your contemplation. For it is precisely in the recovery of our union with our brothers in Christ that we discover God and know Him: for then His life begins to penetrate our souls and His love possesses our faculties and we are able to find out Who He is from the experience of His own selflessness reflected in our purified wills."

SEEDS OF CONTEMPLATION, 49

"The poet enters himself in order to create. The contemplative enters into God in order to be created."

SEEDS OF CONTEMPLATION, 65

IT DRAWS ME
A4

THE ART OF CONTEMPLATION

A5

Saviour (A. Rublev), early 15th century, TRETYAKOV GALLERY, MOSCOW

IT DRAWS ME
A6

"The being that is given to me is given with certain possibilities which are not open to other beings. And the chief of these possibilities is that I am capable of increasing the intensity and the quality of my act of existence by the free response I make to life.

"And here we come to the root problem of life. My being is given me not simply as an arbitrary and inscrutable affliction, but as a source of joy, growth, life, creativity, and fulfillment. But the decision to take existence only as an affliction is left to me.

"The real root-sin of modern man is that, in ignoring and contemning being, and especially his own being, he has made his existence a disease and an affliction. And, strangely, he has done this with all kinds of vitalistic excuses, proclaiming at every turn that he stands on the frontiers of new abundance and permanent bliss."

CONJECTURES OF A GUILTY BYSTANDER, 221

IT DRAWS ME

Detail from *Holy Trinity* Icon

THE ART OF CONTEMPLATION
A9

The Assumption of Our Lady, early 13th century, TRETYAKOV GALLERY, MOSCOW

"'The business of every God-fearing man,' says Gandhi, 'is to dissociate himself from evil in total disregard of the consequences. He must have faith in a good deed producing only a good result...He follows the truth though the following of it may endanger his very life. He knows that it is better to die in the way of God than to live in the way of Satan.'"

MY NON-VIOLENCE

"This is precisely the attitude we have lost in the West, because we have lost our fundamentally religious view of reality, of being and of truth. And that is what Gandhi retained. We have sacrificed the power to apprehend and respect what man is, what truth is, what love is, and have replaced them with a vague confusion of pragmatic notions about what can be done with this or that, what is permissible, what is feasible, how things can be used, irrespective of any definite meaning or finality contained in their very nature, expressing the truth and value of that nature."

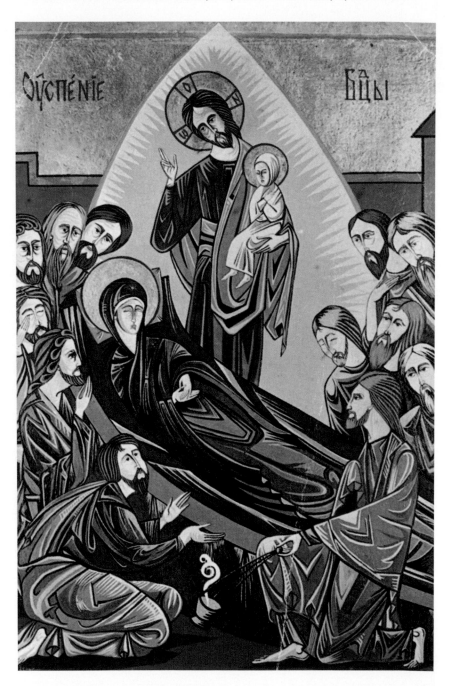

THE ART OF CONTEMPLATION
A13

IT DRAWS ME

A14

THE ART OF CONTEMPLATION
A15

IT DRAWS ME

A16

THE ART OF CONTEMPLATION

Orchids by Ma Lin, 10th century, NEW YORK METROPOLITAN MUSEUM OF ART

IT DRAWS ME
A18

"Solitude as act: the reason no one really understands solitude, or bothers to try to understand it, is that it appears to be nothing but a condition. Something one elects to undergo, like standing under a cold shower. Actually, solitude is a realization, an actualization, even a kind of creation, as well as a liberation of active forces within us, forces that are more than our own, and yet more ours than what appears to be 'ours.' As a mere condition, solitude can be passive, inert, and basically unreal: a kind of permanent coma. One has to work to keep out of this condition....

"Knowing is just a matter of registering that something is objectively verifiable—whether one bothers to verify it or not. Realization is not verification but 'isness.' For this, solitude is necessary, and solitude itself is the fullness of realization. In solitude I become fully able to realize what I cannot know."

LEARNING TO LOVE, 320-321

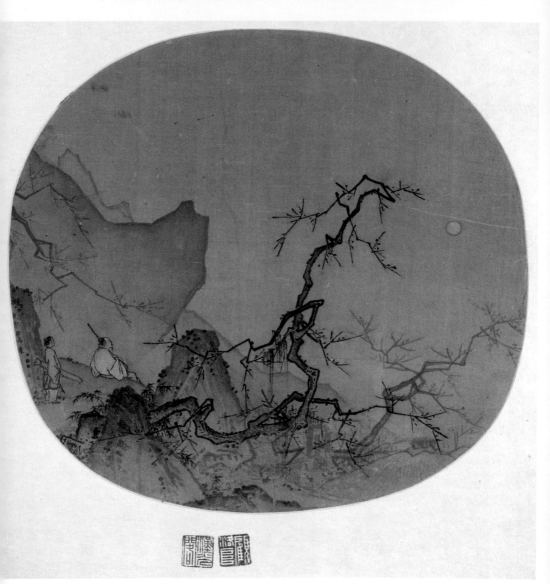

Autumn Moon on Dongting Lake, early 13th century, FREER GALLERY, WASHINGTON, D.C.

IT DRAWS ME

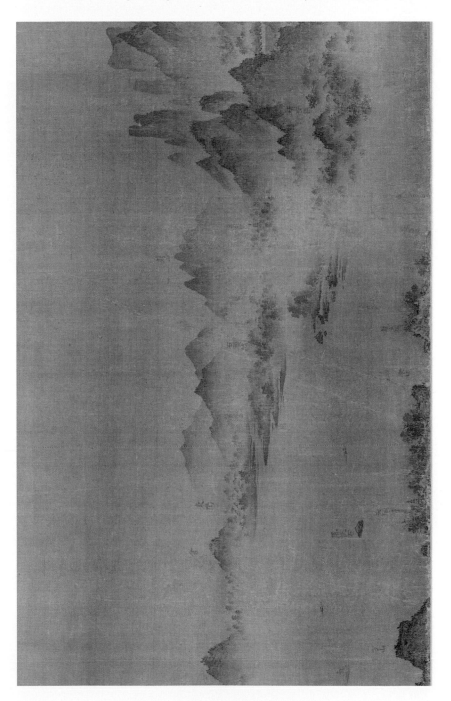

THE ART OF CONTEMPLATION

"The soul that picks and pries at itself in the isolation of its own dull self-analysis arrives at a self-consciousness that is a torment and a disfigurement of our whole personality. But the spirit that finds itself above itself in the intensity and cleanness of its reaction to a work of art is 'self-conscious' in a way that is productive as well as sublime. Such a one finds in himself totally new capacities for thought and vision and moral action. Without a moment of self-analysis he has discovered himself in discovering his capacity to respond to a value that lifts him above his normal level. His very response makes him better and different. He is conscious of a new life and new powers, and it is not strange that he should proceed to develop them."

NO MAN IS AN ISLAND, 34-35

IT DRAWS ME

Landscape With Woodcutters Returning Home, **11th century,** <small>CLEVELAND MUSEUM OF ART</small>

IT DRAWS ME
A28

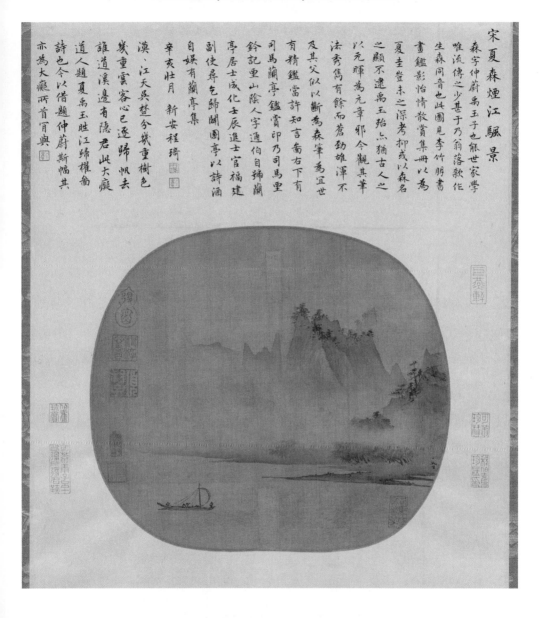

IT DRAWS ME
A30

"Having lost our ability to see life as a whole, to evaluate conduct as a whole, we no longer have any relevant context into which our actions are to be fitted, and therefore all our actions become erratic, arbitrary, and insignificant. To the man who concerns himself only with consequences everything soon becomes inconsequential, nothing 'follows from' anything else, all is haphazard, futile, and absurd. For it is not humanly possible to live a life without significance and remain healthy. A human life has to have a human meaning, or else it becomes morally corrupt."

"The work of writing can be for me, or very close to, the simple job of being....For me to write is love: it is to inquire and to praise, or to confess, or to appeal. This testimony of love remains necessary. Not to assure myself that I am ('I write therefore I am'), but simply to pay my debt to life, to the world, to other men. To speak out with an open heart and say what seems to me to have meaning. The bad writing I have done has all been authoritarian, the declarations of musts, and the announcements of punishments. Bad because it implies a lack of love, good insofar as there may yet have been some love in it. The best stuff has been more straight confession and witness."

LEARNING TO LOVE, POSTSCRIPT

IT DRAWS ME

Academies of the Song Dynasty taught various facets of the three religious or philosophical traditions because they were all so fused in actual daily life. Academies were often founded on Buddhist or Taoist sites,[118] and their initial purpose was to collect books.[119] They incorporated local deities because of their belief that these figures influenced the land itself;[120] and educational philosophies were deeply influenced by Confucian thinking.[121] As Linda Walton writes, "Highly educated abbots and monks moved easily in the world of the Confucian scholar-official, both at court and among their counterparts in areas where large temples and monasteries were located."[122] From her study of academy inscriptions, she found that academies also presented scholars with models of behavior that went beyond the local deities: scholars who held to virtuous paths even in the face of resistance (such as firing) were featured in statues.[123]

What they were learning was called True Way learning, which referred to "the notion that ideas are inscribed with meaning through social practice: in the concrete material existence of people's lives."[124] Much like *lectio divina*, True Way learning emphasized the application of learning. Walton points out that learning was experiential for Confucian thinkers. The teacher was a moral example, and character was a major part of education.[125] Students who became government officials were meant to be models of moral behavior and to transmit their culture through artwork.[126] Academies also promoted "self-cultivation" over worldly status "in order to realize 'original mind' inherent in people as their heaven-endowed human nature."[127] Students were to become sages, much as monks take a vow of conversion of manners. The emphasis was on the development of the self[128] in order to foster peace within the community and peace within the soul because it was in harmony with the divine.

Brushwork as Revealing
the Essence of Things

When brushwork was taught, it was not solely technique, although great technique exists in manuals. Rather, the artist had serious and broad guidelines that came from art critics and even from the emperor. As Wucius Wong writes, the merging of the *Tao* (what) with *Li* (how and why) was the great concern of the neo-Confucian metaphysics of the Song Dynasty. Therefore, to communicate the spirit of something in nature with brush strokes, spaces, and textures was far more important than simply reproducing the subject of the painting.[129] Iconographers, likewise, do not seek to replicate a saint.

The advice that the painter received stemmed from this desire to have paintings communicate a spiritual experience. Nowhere is this desire clearer than in the writing of painter Ching Ho (c. 900-960) and the words of Emperor Huizong. Ching Ho believed that an artist could commit two faults. The first one was a simple error of unrealistic proportion where the viewer is asked to look at a flower bigger than a horse, for instance. Yet the second is the telling one: superficiality was considered the ultimate flaw. Lifeless brushwork and ink, the lack of spirit and harmony—these were elements that made Ching Ho deem a picture not just badly done, but dead.[130]

Emperor Huizong echoed these words when he advised painters in academies to paint their subjects realistically through close observation and to develop alongside their careful observations a poetic feel for their subjects. To communicate that poetic rendering of the subject was the great hope he held out to these painters.[131] This emphasis on not being superficial is such an important part of the training of the artist in this dynasty.

Painting instruction was based on the six canons of Hsieh Ho, the first of which tells artists that vibrancy within painting comes from the artist's own connection with spirit. This spirit is the source of movement within the painting. Sherman E. Lee writes that the artists did not just paint, they used the spirit within to move the wrist, arm, and body. The movement viewers see in Chinese brush strokes originated in the rhythmic movement that the artists had developed over many years of training and painting.[132] The other five canons are as follows: use the brush to create structure; according to the object draw its form; according to the nature of the object apply color; organize the composition with the elements in their proper places; and, in copying, seek to pass on the essence of the master's brush and methods.[133]

The power attributed to the brush itself comes from the respect given to the materials used in painting. Mai Mai Sze writes, "The materials of Chinese painting—brush, ink, inkstone, paper—are the same as the simple equipment on the table in a scholar's study. Always held in deep respect, they have long been called wen fang ssu pao (four treasures of the abodes of culture). Each is dependent on the other, and all are highly prized."[134] Training in calligraphy increased a painter's precision.[135]

The use of color, according to both Sze and Lee, was spare because "ink tones and brush strokes have more telling powers of suggestion than the use of color, an embellishment that, by distracting, can actually be an obstacle to successful results."[136] Lee refers to Wang Hui, who advised that when artists select the perfect set of light and dark together, the spiritual energy would follow.[137] Further, the brush and the ink were considered yang and yin respectively,[138] and color would add more to this balance. Painters received years of training, but it was not unusual for a painter to wait until he was in his fifties to show his artwork.[139]

Each of these ideas concerning brushwork can be seen in the calligraphs drawn by Thomas Merton when he, like the Chinese artists, was in his fifties. The vital movement that the first canon advises was what Merton wanted in his calligraphs. In the essay "Signatures" in *Raids on the Unspeakable*, Merton defends the abstract drawings as beyond interpretation: "ciphers of energy, acts or movements intended to be propitious."[140] His hope for the drawings, like that of Chinese artists, was that they would stand alone, making a viewer aware of life itself, perhaps adding to reflections that the viewer might already have taking place.[141] Inspired by Zen calligraphy, Merton used the brush in the same way that Asian artists did—not as a way to represent something but as a way of affirming life itself and creating awareness of life itself.

His calligraphs echo the Chinese sentiment regarding vitality and uselessness. Merton's translation of Chuang Tzu—especially the poem that venerates the withered old tree as surviving solely out of its uselessness—captures the merging of traditions. As Richard Barnhart writes in *Wintry Forests, Old Trees*, "In their separate ways the Confucian and Buddhist see in the old tree a human image of integrity, dignity, and enduring strength oblivious to the superficial standards of value. Joined to the Taoist Chunag-tzu's ideal of 'uselessness,' these philosophical speculations made of the old tree a powerful and eloquent symbol that never lost its appeal."[142] These old trees, just as Song landscape paintings as a whole, served a special purpose for scholars in exile in future dynasties. They appealed likewise to Merton, whose status as a monk placed him voluntarily in exile, and in contrast to the world, as "useless," even as his brushwork proclaimed his joy in living. His calligraphs can now be found in one volume, that of Roger Lipsey, *Angelic Mistakes: The Art of Thomas Merton*.

The Artist as a Contemplative

The artist acted as a contemplative in three different ways. Like the artists using *lectio divina*, Chinese landscape painters were expected to be contemplatives so that the connection with the life force that they themselves possessed would come through in the paintings. Merton described this experience as indicative of a great work of art: The artist "worked passively" when the Tao was "in and through him."[143]

The extent of the education of the painter is perhaps most interesting. Even if we might have known that the artist was a contemplative, the formation of the artist on so many levels shows us how little our own students receive. As Sze writes,

> In acquiring the education prescribed by the tao of painting, a painter went through rigorous intellectual discipline and intensive training of memory. He acquired a store of knowledge crowned by the essence of Chinese thought—the ideals and ideas of painting comprehensible to all who had the same training as well as to all whose education came through custom and hearsay. The ancient wisdom molded his character and nourished his innermost resources. In writing with brush and ink, he acquired sensitivity and control of his medium, and, because of the nature of Chinese writing, the finest training of hand and eye. Writing Chinese characters also developed a fine sense of proportion, which, in painting, was evident in the arrangement of a composition and its details, in drawing with a brush, and more subtly, in the exercise of taste and discrimination. Such a sense is a form of that sense of fitness, so prominent in every aspect of Chinese life, which Confucius rated as one of the Five Cardinal Virtues. He used the ancient term *li*, generally translated "ritual," although its significance lay rather in the motives and ideas underlying ritual.[144]

Beyond the description that Sze gives, the artist worked within a culture that also valued the merging of spirit (heaven) and matter (earth) as part of the *tao* of living, such that the painting captured both, as did the painter himself.[145]

The training of the Chinese artist parallels that of iconographers and of Merton himself. All had a very firm grasp of the fundamentals of their art form; Merton was a voracious reader in boarding schools. He never let go of his concern that monks read at very basic, careful levels before they attempted challenging texts. Each of these artists as well had the purpose of training or education as the shaping of the inner person. Reading, writing, and art served this purpose. Finally, the support of the culture around them made their art and writing valuable.

At this period in history, the values espoused by Chinese academies paralleled those of Western monasticism. It is no wonder that the art produced by artists in both cultures share so many qualities. Both groups venerated their ancestors, whose models of behavior were used as examples. Both saw contemplation in nature as a way of connecting with the divine. Both understood the value of placing their institutions within grounds that were beautiful and at some distance to cities. Both cherished learning not for its own sake, but for the cultivation of character and sagacity. Both saw that any work produced had to be the fruit of the individual person who deemed his connection with the divine as the most vital aspect to his work. Finally, both cultures placed tremendous value on the products of reading, writing, learning, and contemplation and all the smaller aspects of these ventures, even the quality of ink, because even the smallest aspects had the power to convey values they wished to share with a like-minded community.

What Monastic Contemplative Artists Want to Give Us

In a nutshell, these artists wanted peace for viewers—peace that comes from increased faith, courage, protection, silence, renewed relationships, insight, and more. In gathering commonalities in these three forms of art, I hope to give a name to what readers have already experienced or to encourage readers to view or read monastic contemplative art specifically for these gifts. The only requirement for them is the solitude needed to listen, reflect, and apply. That solitude might ideally come during brief periods at morning and night—as Psalm 1 recommends—where readers, like their monastic companions, select a very brief passage of Scripture on which to meditate. Many books are suggested in "Further Reading" for developing this practice of sacred reading.

The heart of monastic prayer is this reflection on Scripture. Reflecting on artwork or the writings of Merton are excellent practices that will work most fully when accompanied by sacred reading. The reflection questions below aim at helping readers identify monastic gifts through both practices.

Interactivity

While most readers feel comfortable with the idea of God's addressing them through readings at church or through feelings during prayer, they can frequently see writing or artwork as flat or inert. It might take some imagination to get used to this conception, but monks view writing and icons as interactive. For the Catholic monk, Scripture is as alive as a voice speaking directly to the hearer, asking him or her to consider various moral decisions. The word "listen" opens *The Rule of Saint Benedict*, signaling this interactivity; the monastic had to work the text through mind and heart and apply it to his or her life. Similarly, in the Song Dynasty, the painter knew that the presence of the life force, painted often as the space that takes up the greatest part of the scroll, was living and active. The artists themselves were contemplatives conveying that experience to others. There was an interactivity between themselves and God or the life force that was a vital part of what they wished to convey.

For Reflection

* *When I bring the concept of interactivity with me to Scripture or a work of art, what do I see that passage or artwork saying back to me?*

* *Is there some moral decision that I have to make that this interactivity bears on?*

* *How can I experience more oneness with Christ in liturgy as I pray during Mass?*

Communion With God

If there is one gift that busy readers need most, it is the reorienting that the monk offers; in so many activities, such long hours at work, and great responsibilities, we easily lose focus about our connection with God. The monk is connected to God in contemplation. The Song Dynasty artist was expected to live out a contemplative life as a matter of connection with the mysterious life force. Even though this experience may vary greatly among individuals, the same hope for connection holds.

For Reflection

* *What does artwork or a Scripture passage call me to understand and experience about connection with God?*

* *Are there any changes I would make in my various vocations because of this call to connection in interior silence?*

Connection Within the Self

If we easily lose our focus about our connection with God, we also lose our connection with ourselves. Efforts to serve others as well as balance our own responsibilities can leave us without a sense of how we feel or think about ourselves.

During *lectio divina*, the monastic gains knowledge of him- or herself through reflection on Scripture or through contemplation. The experience of contemplation, as Thomas Keating writes in *Open Mind, Open Heart*, is one that exposes underdeveloped aspects of the self and often points out where a person has to grow. This development of character was a prime motive of artists during the Song Dynasty. Ordering one's thoughts and one's character referred to a desire for wholeness or consistency within oneself.

For Reflection

* *Does this artwork or a select Scripture passage bring back to me parts that I have ignored or neglected?*

* *Does this passage or artwork summon my best self in some way?*

* *Do I have an outlet to review the information about myself that reflection and contemplation bring about (a journal, for instance, or a friend, or counselor, or time to reflect)?*

Connection With Community

Readers may see themselves having various roles in groups, yet they frequently see themselves as individuals who choose to act. The problem with such a view is that we don't often analyze our communities and our behaviors toward them and their behaviors toward us. Once familiar with the monastic way of praying and reflecting with writing and art, we can see the attention monastics give to the connection with community.

The third moment of *lectio divina*, *Oratio*, refers to behavior. Reading Scripture, we can reflect on how the passage relates to the behavior of community or to our own behavior toward members of various communities. The peace of soul that *The Rule of Saint Benedict* or that *lectio divina* promotes very much concerns our peaceful relations with others. Similarly, the Chinese Song Dynasty painters had read *The Four Books* that promoted well-being within community as a function of the interior peace that the monk cultivated. The scholar and the sage were important to the monastic contemplative traditions considered here. They provided wisdom and guidance to all.

For Reflection

* *What does a select piece of art or Scripture passage ask me to consider regarding the communities of which I am a part?*

* *Does my behavior and the behavior of the communities of which I am a part follow the guidelines of Scripture? Are we in right relationships to each other?*

Connection With Nature

Readers might be frequent visitors of monasteries and of parks, but they may not realize that for monks, nature held special lessons and properties. Monks and Song Dynasty artists placed their homes in beautiful landscapes that gave them enough distance from cities to maintain both solitude and reflection. They believed that the landscape and any facet of nature taught about God and revealed God.

For Reflection

* *What does this artwork or a select Scripture passage suggest about my relationship with nature?*

* *What steps can I take to see nature as revealing God? If I am homebound or city bound, how can I encounter nature more?*

Insight

Resolving tension is what insight is frequently about, and art, as Merton wrote, allows people to sense tension they often live with but do not recognize. The Chinese painters knew that living in an urban area brought about a tension that could only be resolved through being in nature itself or through looking at artwork of landscapes.

Another aspect of insight that art yields is perspective shift. Contemplatives' artwork and writing call us to see things from their distanced perspective, which often brings insight. Their greatest gift of perspective, though, comes with their own connection with God.

For Reflection

* *What do I feel dissonant about when I read a passage of Scripture or look at the artwork in this book or at sacred art in churches, museums, etc.?*

* *How is Scripture or artwork giving me the greater perspective I need to resolve this dissonance?*

An Ordered Way of Life

Most readers could never identify with the very highly structured life of a Cistercian monk, but the concept of an ordered way of life is something that monks hold out to us as a way of promoting life within. Monks of both East and West knew that ordering one's life involved a transformation of character that influenced everyone. It meant following the law of God to Christian monks, and it meant tranquility within the self, the home, and the society for Confucians.

For Reflection

* *How does Scripture or artwork show me some aspect of my life that needs ordering or prioritizing?*

An Invitation to Further Contemplation, Silence, and Serenity

It is not unusual for a person to feel drawn to increased silence and serenity while reading contemplative writing or while viewing Song Dynasty landscape paintings. They are designed to foster this experience because of the value both groups placed on the application of knowledge: If contemplative artists experienced silence and serenity, they wanted readers or viewers very much to share that experience on their own.

For Reflection

* *What kind of contemplation, silence, or serenity does this artwork or writing call me toward?*
* *Can I envision the changes in myself (joy and confidence) that will take place if and when I do bring increased contemplation, silence, and serenity into my vocations?*

Healing

We know the contemplative classics of Merton hold special power to put things right spiritually—a form of healing. Near icons in Europe, people have left small silver tokens of arms, legs, and eyes as testimonies to the healings that have taken place due to the intervention of the saint in the icon.

For Reflection

* *Does the artwork being regarded and prayed through point to some area in my life that needs healing?*

* *Does a particular Scripture passage resonate with me and calm or heal my soul?*

* *How would being more silent and contemplative offer healing to my various vocations?*

Protection

When we use a work of art or some contemplative writing to grow closer to God, we are offered protection in two ways—we are reminded of the protection that God offers us, and we are reminded to pray. Icons were said to protect cities. Chinese Song Dynasty landscape painting worked in the other direction: it protected an entire culture of scholars and artists, which meant preserving Chinese culture, when all of China was invaded by Tartars and then Mongols.

For Reflection

* *How does this artwork or Scripture passage point to the protection of God?*

* *What aspect of my faith needs to grow, according to my experience with a Scripture passage or sacred art?*

Conclusion

The spiritual heritages that rest behind the writings of Thomas Merton, icons, and Chinese Song Dynasty landscape paintings encourage readers and viewers to grow in what our busy culture most needs—connection with God, others, nature, and the self; insight into our own and others' behavior; peace, silence, and rest; healing and protection; and an active, loving relationship with God. The contemplative artist—in his or her own quiet way—urges us toward these healing principles for our own well-being and for those in the community alongside of us.

★

Concluding Remarks

Forget your people and your father's house,
that the king might desire your beauty.
He is your lord;
honor him, daughter of Tyre (Psalm 45:11–13).

This psalm is read every Saturday in honor of our Lady during the Divine Office after lunch called None. What is interesting to us, in our consideration of monastic contemplative art, is that beauty in this psalm consists of two interior qualities: forgetting and honoring. If all the king wanted was exterior beauty, we know from later verses that he already sees that she is "arrayed in gold" and her gown has gold embroidery. What the psalmist is highlighting is the ability to redirect attention and to lovingly focus on God.

The ability to realign and redirect (and even transform) is what monastic contemplative artists seek to develop when they compose. Transformation, however, requires "a purified person." Cistercians have long held a special relationship with Mary as the model of such a person and as a protector.[146] To integrate physical beauty (the matter of art) with the spiritual "yes" of Mary is, as Basil M. Pennington wrote, a special feature of Byzantine spirituality, which began the spiritual experiences of Thomas Merton.[147] Pennington writes the following concerning Merton's spiritual development :

> Merton really grows with Evagrius Ponticus and Maximus and John Cassian to see that the purified person is a conduit for God's light and action. Transformation of the world is possible only to purified people. You eventually get to finding our true place in the life of the Trinity.[148]

Only Mary is that purified person, and yet we all strive for that purification in the great and small areas of our lives. Art can help us move in those directions. It can remind us directly of the salvation of Christ, or indirectly of the stories of saints or of the clemency of our Lady. It can foster a dissonance within that causes us to pay attention to some neglected area of our lives. This neglected area can be a place for healing and reflection, and it can be something we need to explore more in prayer. It can be something of joy as well, in that something in us is good but underdeveloped.

The monastic contemplative artist seeks to place our attention back on God, because when we do that, we are not shaken, as Psalm 46 reminds us. The waters of contemplation flow under the city of God and it will not be disturbed. When we allow ourselves to be shaped by an icon or a drawing or a work of writing, we allow those waters to flow in our hearts and minds, enabling us to prioritize and to do God's will. We can forget old ways and honor God.

The fruitfulness of this realignment, redirection, and action is so clear when we examine the results of the traditions studied here. The contemplative classics of Thomas Merton inspired millions when Merton published them in the years between the end of World War II and December 10, 1968, when he died. These were momentous, turbulent years, and the work of Merton comforted and redirected many. Merton was able to pose current views of various important issues (freedom, for instance) alongside a spiritual view of the same thing, which allowed readers to form their own opinions—a marvelous rhetorical tactic to help people see spiritual things. Merton allowed readers to feel respected, not pressured. They could forget their old way of seeing something and honor a more spiritual view.

When we study the work of iconographers, we see that they verify the ability of artists to hold the world of matter together with the world of spirit and to encourage those who view icons to treasure both. They foster the need for the inner sobriety discussed in *The Philokalia*. Their art juxtaposes the black and gold to emphasize our need for salvation and our anticipation of the great joy of communion with God.

The Chinese of the Song Dynasty preserved their entire literate culture through their works of art. Their conquering enemies retained their culture. Even though great sadness followed the loss of the *shih* culture, this artwork remains to this day an enduring testimony to the power of the contemplation that shaped it. The Chinese artists sought to encourage good character through the reflection of nature.

Each of these contemplative monastic communities created artwork that eventually created great peace for the individual and the community. Neglecting to study the spiritual heritages that formed these artworks would be to neglect the great depth of help these artworks have given to communities. It would also mean to neglect the messages that the artists gave that were codes to the spiritual life. These artworks are somewhat subtle in their messages, yet the Catholic of today should know the richness of these messages so as to more greatly appreciate them and to carry their meanings into his or her own daily life.

Further Reading on
Contemplative Spirituality

Baggley, John. *Doors of Perception: Icons and Their Spiritual Significance.*Crestwood, NY: Saint Vladimir's Seminary Press, 1987.
To understand icons more fully, readers will find that this book presents a variety of icons with their historical and spiritual explanations after discussing the history and spirituality of icons in general.

Casey, Michael. *Sacred Reading.* Liguori, MO: Liguori/Triumph, 1996.
Readers will find this wonderful book presents lectio divina *as a way to renew or refresh faith; it gives historical background and practical instruction.*

Casey, Michael. *Toward God.* Liguori, MO: Liguori/Triumph, 1996.
A wonderful study on contemplative prayer in a variety of dimensions.

Chittister, Joan. *Wisdom Distilled from the Daily: Living the Rule of Saint Benedict Today.* San Francisco: HarperSanFrancisco, 1990.
Taking monastic values from The Rule of Saint Benedict, *Chittister shows readers how to apply them to daily life.*

Doherty, Catherine De Heuck. *Molchanie: The Silence of God.* New York: Crossroad, 1982.
Silence as a vocation—a mystical book on Russian spirituality.

Doherty, Catherine De Heuck. *Poustinia: Christian Spirituality of the East for Western Man.* Notre Dame, IN: Ave Maria Press, 1975.
A remarkable book for its clarity about the ability to dwell in peace through allowing God to cleanse the soul in solitude; the Russian spirituality behind this practice is explained.

International Association of Lay Cistercian Contemplatives. "Welcome." http://cistercianfamily.org/, 2012.
This website allows readers to find both lay contemplative groups and monasteries that host them. The association offers meetings. The website also gives links to important Cistercian documents.

Keating, Thomas. *Open Mind, Open Heart: The Contemplative Dimension of the Gospel.* New York: Continuum, 2000.
This book encompasses what happens to a person when he or she embarks on contemplative prayer.

Louf, Andre. *The Cistercian Way.* Translated by Nivard Kinsella. Kalamazoo, MI: Cistercian Publications, 1989.
The full life of the Cistercian explained through the values of the order.

Louf, Andre. *Teach Us to Pray*. Translated by Hubert Hoskins. Cambridge, MA: Cowley
Publications, 1992.
A very helpful book regarding contemplative prayer through discussion of Scripture and experience.

Manss, Virginia, and Mary Frohlich, eds. *The Lay Contemplative*. Cincinnati: Saint Anthony
Messenger Press, 2000.
Readers can find lists of lay contemplative groups here as well as chapters devoted to the lay contemplative experience.

Merton, Thomas. *Contemplative Prayer*. New York: Image, 1990.
Merton, Thomas. *New Seeds of Contemplation*. New York: New Directions, 1961.

Nouwen, Henri. *Behold the Beauty of the Lord: Praying With Icons*. Notre Dame, IN: Ave
Maria Press, 1987.
Reflections and explanations of icons from a great spiritual writer.

Robertson, Duncan. *Lectio Divina: The Medieval Experience of Reading*. Kalamazoo, MI:
Cistercian Publications, 2011.
To see all the medieval and important commentaries in one book on this subject is wonderful.

Vest, Norvene. *No Moment Too Small: Rhythms of Silence, Prayer, and Holy Reading*. Kalamazoo, MI: Cistercian Publications, 1994.
An insightful, practical way into contemplative prayer, thoughtfully written.

Vest, Norvene. *Preferring Christ: A Devotional Commentary and Workbook on The Rule of
Saint Benedict*. Trabuco Canyon, CA: Source Books, 1990.
A wonderful way to begin lectio divina, *as the book has space for writing.*

Bibliography

Alpatov, M.V. *Treasures of Russian Art in the 11th–16th Centuries*. Leningrad:Aurora Art Publishers, 1971.

Aprile, Diane. *The Abbey of Gethsemani*. Louisville, KY: Trout Lily Press, 1998.

Baggley, John. *Doors of Perception: Icons and Their Spiritual Significance*.Crestwood, NY: Saint Vladimir's Seminary Press, 1987.

Baidu Encyclopedia. "Hui Inksticks." http://tieba.baidu.com/f?kz=570949882.

Bamberger, John Eudes. "Thomas Merton: Reflections on the Way of Prayer." Cistercian Studies 45, No. 1 (2010): 63–86.

Barnhart, Richard. *Along the Border of Heaven: Sung and Yuan Paintings*. New York: Metropolitan Museum of Art, 1983.

Barnhart, Richard. *Plum Blossom Spring*. New York: Metropolitan Museum of Art, 1983.

Barnhart, Richard. *Wintry Forests, Old Trees*. New York: China Institute of America, 1972.

Beckett, Wendy, Sister. *The Gaze of Love: Meditations on Art and Spiritual Transformation*. San Francisco: HarperSanFrancisco, 1993.

Bender, Sue. *Plain and Simple*. San Francisco: HarperSanFrancisco, 1989.

Benedict, Saint. *The Rule of Saint Benedict in English*. Ed. Timothy Fry, OSB, Collegeville, MN: Liturgical College Press, 1981.

Bol, Peter. *"This Culture of Ours": Intellectual Tradition in T'ang and Sung China*. Stanford, CA: Stanford University Press, 1992.

Cahill, James. *The Art of Southern Sung China*. New York: Asia House, 1976.

Cahill, James. *The Painter's Practice*. New York: Columbia University Press, 1994.

Casey, Michael. *Sacred Reading*. Liguori, MO: Liguori/Triumph, 1996.

Ch'eng-Wu, Fei. *Brush Drawing in the Chinese Manner*. London: Studio Publications, 1957.

Chittister, Joan. *Wisdom Distilled From the Daily*. San Francisco: HarperSanFrancisco, 1990.

Contemplative Outreach. "Front Page." Contemplative Outreach, Ltd. centeringprayer.com/frntpage.htm.

Coomler, David. *The Icon Handbook*. Springfield, IL: Templegate, 1995.

Cunningham, Lawrence S. *Thomas Merton and the Monastic Vision*. Grand Rapids, MI: W.B. Eerdsmans Publications, 1999.

Doherty, Catherine De Heuck. *Molchanie: The Silence of God*. New York: Crossroad, 1982.

Doherty, Catherine De Heuck. *Poustinia: Christian Spirituality of the East for Western Man*. Notre Dame, IN: Ave Maria Press, 1975.

Dillon, Christopher. "*Lectio Divina* in the Monastic Tradition," *Cistercian Studies Quarterly* 34 (1999): 311–320.

Frances, James. "Cistercians Under Our Lady's Mantle." *Cistercian Studies Quarterly* 37, No. 4 (2002): 393–414.

Franck, Frederick. *The Zen of Seeing: Seeing/Drawing as Meditation.* New York: Vintage, 1973.

Fong, Wen. *Sung and Yuan Paintings.* New York: Metropolitan Museum of Art, 1973.

Goleman, Daniel. *Destructive Emotions: How Can We Overcome Them?* New York: Audio Renaissance, 2003.

Goepper, Roger. *The Essence of Chinese Painting.* Translated by Michael Bullock. London: Percy Lund, Humphries, & Co, Ltd., 1963.

Grousset, Rene. *The Art of the Far East: Landscapes, Flowers, Animals.* New York: Oxford University Press, 1936.

Hearn, Maxwell K. *Splendors of Imperial China: Treasures from the National Palace Museum,* Taipei. New York: Metropolitan Museum of Art, 1996.

"Hui Inkstick—2nd Artist's Treasure." Acorn Planet. acornplanet.com/hui inkstick.shtml

Keating, Thomas. "The Classical Monastic Practice of *Lectio Divina*." Contemplative Outreach News 12, No. 2 (1998): 1–2.

Keating, Thomas. *Open Mind, Open Heart.* New York: Continuum, 2000.

Kristoff, Donna, Sister "'The Light That Is Not Light': Thomas Merton and the Icon." *Merton Annual.* Edited by Robert E. Daggy, Patrick Hart, OCSO, Dewey Weiss Kramer, Victor A. Kramer, 85–117. New York: AMS Press, 1989.

Lai, T.C. *Chinese Painting: Its Mystic Essence.* Kowloon, Hong Kong: Swindon Book Co., 1974.

Leclerq, Jean. *The Love of Learning and the Desire for God.* Translated by Catharine Misrahi. New York: Fordham University Press, 1961.

Lee, Sherman E. *The Colors of Ink: Chinese Paintings and Related Ceramics From the Cleveland Museum of Art.* New York: Asia Society, Inc., 1974.

Lee, Sherman E., and Wen Fong. *Streams and Mountains without End: A Northern Sung Handscroll and Its Significance in the History of Early Chinese Painting.* 2nd ed. Ascona, Switzerland: Artibus Asiae Publishers, 1966.

Levi, Yehudah. *Torah Study: A Survey of Classic Sources on Timely Issues.* Translated by Raphael N. Levi. Jerusalem: Philipp Feldheim, 1990.

Lipsey, Roger. *Angelic Mistakes: The Art of Thomas Merton.* Boston: New Seeds, 2006.

Loehr, Max. *The Great Painters of China.* New York: Harper & Row, 1980.

Lonergan, Bernard. *Insight: A Study in Human Understanding.* 1957. New York: Philosophical Library, 1978.

Louf, Andre. *The Cistercian Way.* Kalamazoo, MI: Cistercian Publications, 1983.

Merton, Thomas. *Conjectures of a Guilty Bystander.* New York: Image, 1965.

Merton, Thomas. *Contemplative Prayer.* New York: Image, 1969.

Merton, Thomas. *Entering the Silence.* Journals 2; 1941–1952. Ed. Jonathan Montaldo. San Francisco: HarperSanFrancisco, 1996.

Merton, Thomas. *Learning to Love: Exploring Solitude and Freedom.* The Journals, Vol. 6, 1966-1967. Edited by Christine M. Bochen. San Francisco: HarperSanFrancisco, 1997.

Merton, Thomas. *"Lectio Divina."* n.d. Thomas Merton Center. Bellarmine University Library. Bellarmine University, Louisville, KY.

Merton, Thomas. *My Argument With the Gestapo*. 1941. New York: New Directions, 1969.

Merton, Thomas. *No Man Is an Island*. New York: New Directions, 1965.

Merton, Thomas. *Run to the Mountain*. Journals 1; 1939–1941. Ed. Patrick Hart, OCSO. San Francisco: HarperSan Francisco, 1995.

Merton, Thomas. *Seeds of Contemplation*. New York: Dell, 1949.

Merton, Thomas. "Signatures," in *Raids on the Unspeakable*. New York: New Directions, 1966, 179–182.

Merton, Thomas. *The Sign of Jonas*. New York: Harcourt, Brace, Jovanovich, 1953.

Merton, Thomas. *The Waters of Siloe*. New York: Harcourt Brace, 1949.

Merton, Thomas. *The Way of Chuang Tzu*. New York: New Directions, 1965.

Miles, Margaret. *Image as Insight*. Boston: Beacon Press, 1985.

Mott, Michael. *The Seven Mountains of Thomas Merton*. Boston: Houghton Mifflin,1984.

Nouwen, Henri. *Behold the Beauty of the Lord: Praying with Icons*. Notre Dame, IN: Ave Maria Press, 1988.

Onasch, Konrad. *Russian Icons*. Translated by I. Grafe. Oxford, England: Phaidon Press, 1977.

Ouspensky, Leonid. *Theology of the Icon*. Vols. 1 & 2. Translated by Anthony Gythiel. Crestwood, NY: Saint Vladimir's Seminary Press, 1992.

Ouspensky, Leonid and Vladimir Lossky. *The Meaning of Icons*. Crestwood, NY: Saint Vladimir's Seminary Press, 1982.

Pelikan, Jaroslav. *Imago Dei: The Byzantine Apologia for Icons*. Princeton, NJ: Princeton University Press, 1990.

Pennington, Basil M. *Lectio Divina*. New York: Crossroad, 1998.

Philokalia: The Complete Text. Compiled by Saint Nikodimus of the Holy Mountain and Saint Makarios of Corinth. Translated and edited by G.E.H. Palmer, Philip Sherard, Kallistos Ware. London: Faber & Faber, 1979.

Richards, M.C. *Centering in Pottery, Poetry, and the Person*. 2nd ed. Middletown, CT: Wesleyan University Press, 1989.

Robertson, Duncan. *Lectio Divina: The Medieval Experience of Reading*. Collegeville, MN: Cistercian Publications, 2011.

Sendler, Egon, SJ. *The Icon: Image of the Invisible*. Torrance, CA: Oakwood Publications, 1993.

Sherrard, Philip. *The Sacred in Life and Art*. Ipswich, England: Golgonooza Press, 1990.

Siren, Osvald. *The Chinese on the Art of Painting: Tradition and Comments*. Peiping: Henri Vetch, 1936. Reprint, Mineola, NY: Dover Publications, 2005.

Sofukawa, Hiroshi. "The Song Dynasty." *Chinese Painting*, ed. Torao Miyagawa, 119–128. New York: Weatherhill, 1983.

Stuart, John. *Ikons*. London: Faber & Faber, 1975.

Swan, Laura. *The Forgotten Desert Mothers*. New York: Paulist Press, 2001.

Sze, Mai Mai. *The Tao of Painting*, Vol. 1. New York: Pantheon, 1956.

Taki, Sei-Ichi. *Three Essays on Oriental Painting*. London: BernardQuaritch, 1910.

Temple, Richard. "Silence of the Heart." *Parabola* 15, No. 2 (1990): 28–36.

Vandier-Nicolas, Nicole. *Chinese Painting: An Expression of a Civilization.* Translated by Janet Seligman. New York: Rizzoli, 1983.

Vest, Norvene. *No Moment Too Small.* Kalamazoo, MI: Cistercian, 1994.

Walton, Linda. *Academies and Society in Southern Sung China.* Honolulu: University of Hawaii Press, 1999.

Wong, Wucius. *The Tao of Chinese Landscape Painting.* New York: Design Press, 1991.

Endnotes

1. Father Francis Steger, OCSO, "Re: After Vigils," personal e-mail (December 8, 2001) and Father Marcellus Earl, OCSO, personal e-mail (November 3, 2011).
2. Father John Eudes Bamberger, OCSO. "Re: After Vigils," June 28, 2001, personal e-mail (June 30, 2001).
3. Thomas Merton, *The Sign of Jonas* (New York: Harcourt Brace Jovanovich, 1953), 63.
4. Thomas Merton, *Entering the Silence* (Journals 2; 1941–1952), ed. Jonathan Montaldo (San Francisco: HarperSanFrancisco, 1996), 63.
5. Merton, *Entering*, 65.
6. Merton, *Entering*, 65-66.
7. The waters of siloe refer to the stream that flows into the pool of Shiloah in Jerusalem, the slow current of which symbolizes the contemplative life and the protection of God that Judah rejected; this rejection is mentioned in Isaiah 8:6. Merton wrote on the page facing the table of contents of *The Waters of Siloe* that "These are the waters which the world does not know, because it prefers the water of bitterness and contradiction. These are the waters of peace, of which Christ said: 'He that drink of the water that I shall give him, shall not thirst forever. But the water that I shall give him shall become in him a fountain of water, springing up into life everlasting.'"
8. Merton, Thomas. *The Waters of Siloe* (New York: Harcourt Brace, 1949), 180–181.
9. Diane Aprile mentions that before entering Gethsemani, Dom Dunne worked with his father in the printing and book-binding industry and was a voracious reader: "He believed in the power of the written word and sensed the time was right to use it to the monastery's advantage... As Father Louis later recalled, the abbot seemed as exhilarated by [*Seven Storey Mountain*] as he did." (*The Abbey of Gethsemani*, Louisville: Trout Lily Press, 1998),129-130.
10. Chrisopher Dillon, OSB, "*Lectio Divina* in the Monastic Tradition," *Cistercian Studies* 34 (1999): 312.
11. Yehudah Levi, *Torah Study: A Survey of Classical Sources on Timely Issues*, trans. Raphael N. Levi (Jerusalem: Philipp Feldheim, 1990).
12. Dillon, 312.
13. Dillon, 313. See also Laura Swan, *The Forgotten Desert Mothers*. (New York: Paulist Press, 2001), 28.
14. Jean Leclerq, *The Love of Learning and the Desire for God*, trans. Catherine Misrahi (New York: Fordham University Press, 1961), 98.
15. Duncan Robertson, *Lectio Divina: The Medieval Experience of Reading* (Kalamazoo, MI: Cistercian Publications, 2011), 102.
16. Leclerq, 15.
17. *The Rule of Saint Benedict*, 48:17-18.
18. Leclerq, 18.
19. Leclerq, 85.
20. Merton, *Sign*, 59.

21. Thomas Keating, "The Classical Monastic Practice of *Lectio Divina*," *Contemplative Outreach News* 12, no. 2 (1998): 8-12.
22. Mary M. Murray, "Aristotle Meets the Spiritual Classics: The Rhetoric of Thomas Merton," *The Merton Seasonal* 17, no. 2 (1992): 8-12.
23. Mark Meade, "Re: thanks!," March 9, 2009, personal e-mail, Thomas Merton Center, Bellarmine College, Louisville.
24. Thomas Merton. *"Lectio Divina."* n.d. Thomas Merton Center, Bellarmine College, Louisville. 1.
25. Merton, *"Lectio Divina,"* 3.
26. Merton, *"Lectio Divina,"* 7.
27. Merton, *"Lectio Divina,"* 9.
28. Merton, *"Lectio Divina,"* 11.
29. Merton, *"Lectio Divina,"* 25.
30. Merton, *"Lectio Divina,"* 27.
31. Merton, *"Lectio Divina,"* 29.
32. Merton, *"Lectio Divina,"* 29.
33. Merton, *"Lectio Divina,"* 31.
34. Merton, *"Lectio Divina,"* 31.
35. Leclerq, 196.
36. Thomas Keating, *Open Mind, Open Heart* (New York: Continuum, 2000), 21.
37. Keating, "Classical," 2.
38. Dillon, 317.
39. Brother George Fyffe, interview by author. Abbey of the Genesee, Piffard, NY, August 7, 2001.
40. Thomas Merton, *Conjectures of a Guilty Bystander* (New York: Image, 1965), 150.
41. Thomas Merton, *Run to the Mountain: The Story of a Vocation,* ed. Patrick Hart, OCSO. (San Francisco: HarperSanFrancisco, 1995), 97.
42. Merton, *Conjectures,* 117.
43. Merton, *Conjectures,* 117–118.
44. Thomas Merton, *Contemplation in a World of Action* (Notre Dame, IN: University of Notre Dame Press, 1998): 153.
45. Merton, *Contemplation,* 18.
46. Thomas Merton, *Learning to Love,* ed. Christine Bochen (San Francisco: HarperSanFrancisco, 1997), postscript.
47. Job 42:5.
48. Thomas Merton, *Seven Storey Mountain* (New York: Harcourt Brace Jovanovich, 1976), 109.
49. Merton, *Seven,* 109.
50. Merton, *Seven,* 111.
51. Michael Mott, *The Seven Stories of Thomas Merton* (Boston: Houghton Mifflin, 1984), 68.
52. Donna Kristoff, "Light That Is Not Light: A Consideration of Thomas Merton and the Icon," in *Merton Annual* Vol. 2, eds. Robert E. Daggy Patrick Hart, OCSO, Dewey Weiss Kramer, & Victor A. Kramer (New York: AMS Press, 1989), 85–117.

53. Most of the information in this section is taken from John Baggley in his book *Doors of Perception: Icons and Their Spiritual Significance* (Crestwood, NY: Saint Vladimir's Seminary Press, 1987).

54. Henri J.M. Nouwen, *Behold the Beauty of the Lord: Praying with Icons* (Notre Dame, IN: Ave Maria Press, 1988), 13.

55. Baggley, *Doors*, 82.

56. "1st Sunday of Great Lent," The Orthodox Church in America, http://oca.org/FStropars.asp?SID=13&ID=10.

57. Jaroslav Pelikan, *Imago Dei: The Byzantine Apologia for Icons* (Princeton, NJ: Princeton University Press, 1990), 98.

58. Baggley, 77.

59. Egon Sendler, *The Icon: Image of the Invisible* (Torrence, CA: Oakwood Publications, 1993), 76.

60. John Stuart, *Ikons* (London: Faber & Faber, 1975), 36.

61. Stuart, 26.

62. Baggley, 76.

63. Baggley, 83.

64. Sendler, 58–60.

65. Baggley, 64.

66. Baggley, 65.

67. Baggley, 68.

68. Richard Temple, "Silence of the Heart," *Parabola* 15, no. 2 (1990): 34.

69. G.E.H. Palmer, Philip Sherrard, Kallistos Ware, trans. & eds., *The Philokalia: The Complete Text*. Vol. 3. Compiled by Saint Nikodimus of the Holy Mountain and Saint Makarios of Corinth. (London: Faber & Faber, 1979), 30.

70. Temple, 35.

71. Thomas Merton, *Conjectures of a Guilty Bystander* (New York: Image, 1966), 195–196.

72. Leonid Ouspensky, *Theology of the Icon*. Vol. 1. (Crestwood, NY: Saint Vladimir's Seminary Press, 1992), 178.

73. Konrad Onasch, *Russian Icons* (New York: Dutton, 1977), 9.

74. Merton, *Seven Storey Mountain*, 108.

75. Sendler, 239.

76. Stuart, 36.

77. Ouspensky, 166.

78. Baggley, 78.

79. Baggley, 82.

80. Baggley, 88.

81. Baggley, 89.

82. David Coomler, *The Icon Handbook* (Springfield, IL: Templegate, 1995), 25.

83. Coomler, 72.

84. Coomler, 28.

85. M.V. Alpatov, *Treasures of Russian Art in the 11th-16th Centuries (Paintings)* (Leningrad: Aurora Art Publishers, 1971), 8.

86. Baggley, 97.

87. Of course, such beliefs have gone too far, as when icons have been scraped and the paint swallowed to promote healing. H. Daniel-Rops, *The Church in the Dark Ages* (London: J.M. Dent & Sons, 1959), 355.
88. "Hui Inksticks," Baidu Encyclopedia, http://tieba.baidu.com/f?kz=570949882.
89. "Hui Inkstick."
90. "Hui Inkstick."
91. Sherman E. Lee, *The Colors of Ink: Chinese Paintings and Related Ceramics from the Cleveland Museum of Art* (New York: The Asia Society, Inc., 1974), 10.
92. Philippians 4:8.
93. Thomas Merton, *Zen and the Birds of Appetite* (New York: New Directions, 1965), 15.
94. Linda Walton, *Academies and Society in Southern Sung China* (Honolulu: University of Hawaii, 1999), 107.
95. James Cahill, *The Art of Southern Sung China* (New York: Asia House, 1976), 11-12.
96. Max Loehr, *The Great Painters of China* (New York: Harper & Row, 1980), 197.
97. Nicole Vandier-Nicolas, *Chinese Painting: An Expression of a Civilization*, trans. Janet Seligman (New York: Rizzoli, 1983), 106.
98. Vandier-Nicolas, 115.
99. Walton, 108.
100. Walton, 111.
101. Walton, 105.
102. Wucius Wong, *The Tao of Chinese Landscape Painting* (New York: Design Press, 1991), 14.
103. Thomas Merton, *The Way of Chuang Tzu* (New York: New Directions, 1965), 21.
104. Merton, *Way*, 21.
105. Walton, 105.
106. Walton, 18.
107. Walton, 89–91.
108. *The Four Books: Confucian Analects, The Great Learning, The Doctrine of the Mean,* and *The Works of Mencius*, trans. & ed. James Legge (New York: Paragon, 1966), 311–312.
109. Osvald Siren, *The Chinese on the Art of Painting: Translations and Comments* (Peiping, China: Henri Vetch, 1936; Mineola, NY: Dover Publications, 2005), 92.
110. Siren, 93.
111. Siren, 100.
112. Siren, 101.
113. Siren, 105.
114. Peter Bol, *"This Culture of Ours": Intellectual Tradition in T'ang and Sung China* (Stanford, CA: Stanford University Press, 1992), 335.
115. Walton, 198.
116. Maxwell K. Hearn, *The Splendors of Imperial China: Treasures from the National Palace Museum, Taipei* (New York: Metropolitan Museum, 1996), 63.
117. Walton, 200.
118. Walton, 100.
119. Walton, 204.
120. Walton, 105.

121. Walton, 105.

122. Walton, 16.

123. Walton, 202.

124. Walton, 7.

125. Walton, 7, 202.

126. Walton, 11.

127. Walton, 197.

128. Bol, 342.

129. Wong, 18.

130. Fei Ch'eng-wu, *Brush Drawing in the Chinese Manner* (London: Studio Publishers, 1957), 22.

131. Hiroshi Sofukawa, "The Sung Dynasty," in *Chinese Painting*, ed. Torao Miyagawa (New York: Weatherhill, 1983), 125.

132. Lee, 33.

133. Mai Mai Sze, *The Tao of Painting*. Vol. 1. (New York: Pantheon, 1956), 52-53.

134. Sze, 64.

135. Sze, 6.

136. Sze, 75.

137. Lee, 12.

138. Sze, 76.

139. Lee, 11.

140. Thomas Merton, "Signatures" in *Raids on the Unspeakable* (New York: New Directions, 1966), 180.

141. Merton, *Raids*, 182.

142. Richard Barnhart, *Wintry Forests, Old Trees* (New York: China Institute in America, 1972), 10.

143. Merton, *Way*, 31.

144. Sze, 6.

145. Sze, 33.

146. James Frances, "Cistercians Under Our Lady's Mantle," *Cistercian Studies Quarterly* 37, No. 4 (2002): 393-414.

147. Basil M. Pennington, "Thomas Merton and Byzantine Spirituality," in *Toward an Integrated Humanity: Thomas Merton's Spiritual Journey* (Kalamazoo: MI: Cistercian Studies, 1988): 132–136.

148. Pennington, 136–137

Sources and Acknowledgments

EXCERPTS FROM:

The Seven Storey Mountain by Thomas Merton, copyright 1948 by Houghton Mifflin Harcourt Publishing Company and renewed 1976 by the Trustees of The Merton Legacy Trust, reprinted by permission of the publisher. All rights reserved.

The Tao of Painting by Mai Mai Sze courtesy Vintage Books. All rights reserved. Used by permission.

Thomas Merton's unpublished *Lectio Divina Notes*, © Merton Legacy Trust. All rights reserved. Used by permission of the Merton Legacy Trust of New York, with the assistance of The Thomas Merton Center at Bellarmine University, Louisville, KY.

Conjectures of a Guilty Bystander by Thomas Merton, copyright © 1965, 1966 by the Abbey of Gethsemani. Used by permission of Doubleday, a division of Random House, Inc.

The Waters of Siloe, copyright © 1949 by Thomas Merton, copyright renewed 1977 by The Trustees of the Merton Legacy Trust, reprinted by permission of Houghton Mifflin Harcourt Publishing Company Inc.

Learning to Love: The Journals of Thomas Merton, Volume Six 1966-1967 by Thomas Merton and edited by Christine Bochen. Copyright © 1997 by The Merton Legacy Trust. Reprinted by permission of HarperCollins Publishers.

Run to the Mountain: The Journals of Thomas Merton, Volume One 1939-1941 by Thomas Merton and edited by Patrick Hart. Copyright © 1995 by The Merton Legacy Trust. Reprinted by permission of HarperCollins Publishers.

Contemplative Prayer by Thomas Merton, copyright © The Merton Legacy Trust. All rights reserved. Used by permission of the Merton Legacy Trust of New York, with the assistance of The Thomas Merton Center at Bellarmine University, Louisville, KY.

Contemplation in a World of Action by Thomas Merton, copyright © The Merton Legacy Trust. All rights reserved. Used by permission of the Merton Legacy Trust of New York.

The Rule of St. Benedict used by permission of Liturgical Press, Collegeville, MN. All rights reserved.

Wintry Forests, Old Trees by Richard Barnhart, copyright © 1972 by China Institute. All rights reserved. Used by permission of China Institute, New York.

Chinese Painting: An Expression of Civilization by Nicole Vandier-Nicholas, copyright © 1983 by Rizzoli/Universe International Press. All rights reserved. Used by permission of Rizzoli/Universe International Press, New York.

Splendors of Imperial China: Treasures from the National Palace Museum, Taipei by Maxwell K. Hearn, copyright © 1996 by Rizzoli/Universe International Publications. All rights reserved. Used by permission of Rizzoli/Universe International Publication, New York.

Academies and Society in Southern Sung China by Linda Walton, copyright © 1999 by The University of Hawaii Press. All rights reserved. Used by permission of The University of Hawaii Press, Honolulu.

The Chinese Art of Painting: Translations and Comments by Osvald Siren, copyright © 2005 Dover Publications. All rights reserved. Used by permission of Dover Publications, Mineola, NY.

Theology of the Icon by Leonid Ouspensky, copyright © 1992 Saint Vladimir's Seminary Press. All rights reserved. Used by permission of Saint Vladimir's Seminary Press, Yonkers, NY.

The Icon, Image of the Invisible: Elements of Theology, Aesthetics, and Technique by Egon Sendler, copyright © 1993 Oakwood Publications. All rights reserved. Used by permission of Oakwood Publications, Redondo Beach, CA.

Doors of Perception: Icons and Their Spiritual Significance by John Baggley, copyright © 1987 Saint Vladimir's Seminary Press. All rights reserved. Used by permission of Saint Vladimir's Seminary Press, Yonkers, NY.

Kontakion 8, copyright © Orthodox Church in America. All rights reserved. Used by permission of the Orthodox Church in America, Glen Elyn, IL.

By Thomas Merton, from *Raids on the Unspeakable*, copyright © 1966 by The Abbey of Gethsemani, Inc. Reprinted by permission of New Directions Publishing Corp., New York.

By Thomas Merton, from *The Way of Chuang Tzu*, copyright © 1965 by The Abbey of Gethsemani, Inc. Reprinted by permission of New Directions Publishing Corp., New York.

By Thomas Merton, from *Zen and the Birds of Appetite*, copyright © 1968 by The Abbey of Gethsemani, Inc. Reprinted by permission of New Directions Publishing Corp., New York.

By Thomas Merton, from *New Seeds of Contemplation*, copyright © 1961 by The Abbey of Gethsemani, Inc. Reprinted by permission of New Directions Publishing Corp., New York.

Quote from Basil Pennington, copyright © 1987 by Cistercian Publications. All rights reserved. Used by permission of Liturgical Press, Collegeville, MN.

THE IMAGES:

Orchids by Ma Lin and *Viewing Plum Blossoms by Moonlight* by Ma Yuan copyright © The Metropolitan Museum of Art. Art Resource, New York.

Ten Thousand Li Along the Yangtze River, Autumn Moon on Dongting Lake, A Hostelry in the Mountains, Ink Plum Blossoms, and *Pavilion of Rising Clouds*, © Freer Gallery of Art, Smithsonian Institution, Washington, D.C.

Willows, Landscape With Woodcutters, and *Full Sail on Misty River*, © The Cleveland Museum of Art, Cleveland, OH.

Angel Gabriel, © State Russian Museum. Photo Vedit Scala, Art Resource, New York.

Dormition icon from PA, Holy Dormition Monastery, Sybertsville, PA.

Saint Paul the Apostle, Archangel Michael, Our Lady of Great Panagiya, Saviour on a Throne, Holy Trinity, Annunciation, Our Lady of Vladimir, Our Lady of Tolgsk, Transfiguration, Saviour, and *Assumption*, © The State Tretyakov Gallery. All rights reserved. Used by permission of Tretyakov Gallery, Moscow.